Ninja Foodi MAX Dual Zone Air Fryer Cookbook for Beginners UK

2000 Days of Healthy & Delicious Dual Basket Air Fryer Recipes | Easy UK Measurements | Perfect Frying Instructions for Happy Cooking.

Kressida Ishbourne

Table of Contents

INTRODUCTION

Healthy, Delicious, and Low-Fat Cooking with the Ninja Foodi Air Fryer

The Ninja Foodi MAX Dual Zone Air Fryer is revolutionizing the way we cook by offering a healthier alternative to traditional cooking methods without sacrificing flavor. With its innovative design and multiple cooking functions, this appliance makes it easy to create delicious meals with significantly less fat, making it a perfect choice for those looking to maintain a healthy lifestyle.

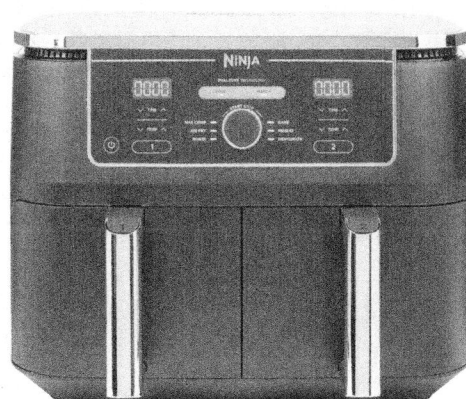

Exploring Healthier Cooking Options:

One of the standout features of the Ninja Foodi MAX Dual Zone Air Fryer is its ability to cook with up to 75% less fat compared to traditional deep frying methods. This is achieved through the use of the Air Fry function, which circulates hot air around the food to produce a crispy exterior without the need for excessive oil. By reducing the amount of oil used in cooking, this appliance helps to lower the overall calorie content of meals, making it easier to maintain a healthy diet.

Additionally, the Air Fry function allows for cooking from frozen to crispy, eliminating the need for pre-frying or preheating frozen foods in oil. This not only saves time but also reduces the amount of oil absorbed by the food during cooking, further enhancing its health benefits.

Nutrient-Rich Cooking with Multiple Functions:

The Ninja Foodi MAX Dual Zone Air Fryer offers six cooking functions, including Max Crisp, Roast, Bake, Reheat, and Dehydrate, in addition to the Air Fry function. Each of these functions provides a unique way to prepare meals, allowing for a wide range of cooking possibilities while still prioritizing health and nutrition.

For example, the Roast function allows for the cooking of meats and vegetables with minimal added fat, helping to retain their natural flavors and nutrients. By utilizing this function, you can create succulent roast chicken or flavorful roasted vegetables without the need for excessive oil or butter.

Similarly, the Dehydrate function enables you to make homemade snacks such as dried fruit or vegetable chips, preserving their nutritional value without the need for added preservatives or oils. This function is particularly useful for those looking to incorporate more whole foods into their diet while reducing their intake of processed snacks.

Cooking for Health and Convenience:

With its extra-large capacity and two independent cooking zones, the Ninja Foodi MAX Dual Zone Air Fryer makes it easy to prepare healthy meals for the whole family with minimal effort. The ability to cook two different foods simultaneously, each with its own cooking function, allows for greater flexibility and convenience in meal preparation.

Whether you're cooking a complete meal in one appliance or catering to different tastes within your household, this feature ensures that everyone can enjoy delicious, healthy food without compromising on flavor or nutrition.

Furthermore, the Ninja Foodi MAX Dual Zone Air Fryer cooks up to 75% faster than traditional fan ovens, making it an ideal choice for busy individuals or families with hectic schedules. With its rapid cooking times and easy-to-use interface, this appliance streamlines the cooking process while still delivering delicious, low-fat meals that everyone will love.

In conclusion, the Ninja Foodi MAX Dual Zone Air Fryer offers a convenient and versatile solution for healthy, delicious, and low-fat cooking. With its innovative design, multiple cooking functions, and extra-large capacity, this appliance makes it easy to prepare nutritious meals for the whole family with minimal effort. Whether you're looking to reduce your intake of unhealthy fats, increase your consumption of whole foods, or simply save time in the kitchen, the Ninja Foodi MAX Dual Zone Air Fryer is sure to exceed your expectations.

Energy Efficiency and Environmental Impact

The Ninja Foodi MAX Dual Zone Air Fryer boasts impressive energy-saving capabilities, promising to reduce energy bills by up to 65% compared to conventional ovens. This claim is substantiated by testing and calculations based on recommended cook times for various foods, particularly sausages. By utilizing its air fry function, this appliance is designed to deliver efficient cooking results while consuming less energy.

Energy efficiency is a critical consideration in today's world, where environmental sustainability is at the forefront of consumer consciousness. Traditional cooking methods often entail preheating large ovens, consuming

substantial amounts of electricity or gas over prolonged periods. In contrast, the Ninja Foodi MAX Dual Zone Air Fryer's ability to cook up to 75% faster than fan ovens, as demonstrated in tests involving fish fingers and sausages, contributes significantly to energy conservation.

Moreover, the appliance's dual-zone design allows for independent cooking in two separate drawers, enabling users to prepare different foods simultaneously. This functionality not only enhances convenience but also contributes to energy efficiency by optimizing the use of cooking space and minimizing the need for multiple appliances.

Reducing energy consumption not only translates to cost savings for consumers but also has a positive environmental impact. By minimizing the amount of electricity or gas required for cooking, the Ninja Foodi MAX Dual Zone Air Fryer helps mitigate greenhouse gas emissions associated with energy production. This aligns with the broader goal of combating climate change and reducing the carbon footprint of household activities.

Furthermore, the appliance's cooking functions, such as Max Crisp, Air Fry, Roast, Bake, Reheat, and Dehydrate, offer versatile options for preparing meals with minimal energy expenditure. The Air Fry function, in particular, is highlighted for its ability to achieve crispy results with up to 75% less fat compared to deep frying, as confirmed in tests involving hand-cut French fries. By promoting healthier cooking methods that require less oil, the Ninja Foodi MAX Dual Zone Air Fryer contributes to environmental sustainability while prioritizing consumer well-being.

In addition to energy efficiency, the appliance's extra-large capacity is noteworthy, as it allows users to cook up to 8 portions in each drawer. This capability reduces the need for multiple cooking sessions and further conserves energy by maximizing the utilization of the appliance's cooking space. Whether preparing a family meal or entertaining guests, the Ninja Foodi MAX Dual Zone Air Fryer offers ample capacity without compromising on efficiency.

Overall, the energy-saving features of the Ninja Foodi MAX Dual Zone Air Fryer, combined with its versatile cooking functions and extra-large capacity, position it as an environmentally conscious choice for modern kitchens. By prioritizing energy efficiency and reducing environmental impact, this appliance aligns with the growing demand for sustainable home appliances that empower consumers to make eco-friendly choices without sacrificing convenience or performance.

Speed and Efficiency with Dual Zone

The Ninja Foodi MAX Dual Zone Air Fryer for the UK market boasts an impressive array of features designed to enhance speed and efficiency in the kitchen. With its innovative dual-zone cooking capability, it revolutionizes the way meals are prepared, offering convenience and versatility like never before.

One of the key highlights of this appliance is its ability to cook two different foods, two different ways, simultaneously. This feature not only saves time but also enables users to cater to diverse tastes and dietary preferences within the same meal. By utilizing different functions, temperatures, and cooking times in each drawer, users can create complete meals in one appliance, eliminating the need for multiple cooking devices and reducing overall cooking time.

The dual-zone cooking also contributes to energy efficiency by optimizing the use of space and resources. Instead of heating up a large oven for small or separate batches of food, users can utilize the independent cooking zones to cook efficiently for smaller portions or different dishes without wasting energy. This targeted approach to cooking helps minimize energy consumption and ultimately

leads to cost savings on energy bills.

Furthermore, the Ninja Foodi MAX Dual Zone Air Fryer offers a range of cooking functions specifically tailored to deliver quick and consistent results. With six cooking functions including Max Crisp, Air Fry, Roast, Bake, Reheat, and Dehydrate, users have the flexibility to prepare a wide variety of dishes with minimal effort. Whether it's crispy fries, succulent roast chicken, or perfectly baked desserts, this appliance delivers delicious results in a fraction of the time compared to conventional cooking methods.

The speed and efficiency of the Ninja Foodi MAX Dual Zone Air Fryer are further exemplified by its extra-large capacity, capable of cooking up to eight portions at once. Each drawer can accommodate up to 1.4kg of fries or a 2kg chicken, making it ideal for feeding large families or entertaining guests. Moreover, the appliance boasts rapid cooking times, cooking up to 75% faster than traditional fan ovens according to testing against common frozen foods like fish fingers and sausages, including preheat time.

Overall, the combination of dual-zone cooking, versatile cooking functions, and extra-large capacity makes the Ninja Foodi MAX Dual Zone Air Fryer a powerhouse in the kitchen when it comes to speed and efficiency. Whether you're whipping up a quick weeknight dinner or hosting a dinner party, this appliance streamlines the cooking process, saving time, energy, and effort without compromising on taste or quality.

Air Fryer Usage Tips

Using an air fryer like the Ninja Foodi MAX Dual Zone Air Fryer can revolutionize your cooking experience, offering healthier alternatives to traditionally fried foods with the added bonus of speed and convenience. To make the most out of your air fryer, here are some usage tips to help you achieve delicious results every time:

Preheat Properly: Just like with a conventional oven, preheating your air fryer is crucial for optimal cooking results. Most air fryers have a preheat function or require a few minutes of preheating before you start cooking. This ensures that your food cooks evenly and crisps up nicely.

Don't Overcrowd: While air fryers offer ample cooking space, it's important not to overcrowd the basket or trays. Leave enough room between food items to allow for proper air circulation. Overcrowding can result in uneven cooking and less crispy results.

Use Oil Wisely: One of the key benefits of air frying is using significantly less oil

than traditional frying methods. However, a light coating of oil can still enhance the flavor and texture of your food. Use a spray bottle or brush to lightly coat your ingredients with oil before air frying. Opt for healthier oils like olive oil or avocado oil.

Experiment with Seasonings: Air frying doesn't just have to be about basic salt and pepper. Get creative with your seasonings and marinades to add flavor to your dishes. Try different spice blends, herbs, citrus zest, or even a sprinkle of Parmesan cheese for a tasty twist.

Flip or Shake: For even cooking, it's a good idea to flip or shake your food halfway through the cooking process. This ensures that all sides are exposed to the circulating hot air, resulting in evenly cooked and crispy food. Use tongs or a spatula to gently flip or shake the contents of the basket or trays.

Monitor Carefully: While air fryers are convenient and efficient, it's still important to monitor your food during the cooking process. Check on your food periodically to ensure that it's cooking evenly and adjust the cooking time or

temperature if necessary.

Use the Right Accessories: Many air fryers come with accessories like racks, trays, or skewers to expand your cooking possibilities. Experiment with different accessories to cook a variety of foods, from kebabs and vegetables to baked goods and even pizza.

Clean Regularly: Proper maintenance is essential for keeping your air fryer in top condition. Make sure to clean the basket or trays, as well as the interior and exterior of the appliance, after each use. Most parts are dishwasher safe, making cleanup a breeze.

Refer to the Recipe Book: Don't be afraid to explore the recipe book that came with your air fryer for inspiration and guidance. It likely contains a variety of recipes specifically tailored for your appliance, along with helpful tips and tricks for successful air frying.

Have Fun and Experiment: Finally, don't be afraid to get creative and experiment with your air fryer. Whether you're trying out new recipes or adapting old

favorites, air frying opens up a world of possibilities for delicious and healthier cooking. Enjoy the process and have fun exploring all that your air fryer can do!

Cleaning and Maintenance

Cleaning and maintenance are essential aspects of owning any kitchen appliance, and the Ninja Foodi MAX Dual Zone Air Fryer is no exception. With its innovative design and multiple cooking functions, keeping it clean ensures optimal performance and longevity. Let's delve into the cleaning and maintenance practices for this appliance.

Firstly, let's discuss the exterior. The exterior of the Ninja Foodi MAX Dual Zone Air Fryer can be wiped down with a damp cloth or sponge. Make sure to unplug the appliance before cleaning and avoid using abrasive cleaners or scouring pads that could scratch the surface. Regular wiping down of the exterior helps prevent the buildup of grease and grime, keeping the appliance looking new for longer.

Moving on to the interior, the cooking drawers and trays are typically made of non-stick materials for easy cleaning. After each use, allow the appliance to cool down completely before removing the cooking drawers. Wash the drawers, trays, and any accessories with warm, soapy water and a non-abrasive sponge or cloth. For stubborn residue, you can soak the parts in warm, soapy water before cleaning.

Avoid using metal utensils or abrasive cleaners on the non-stick surfaces to prevent scratching and damaging the coating. If there are any tough stains or stuck-on food particles, you can use a soft-bristled brush or nylon scrubber to gently remove them. Ensure that all parts are thoroughly dried before reassembling the appliance or storing it away to prevent mold or mildew growth.

Additionally, the heating elements and fan may accumulate grease and debris over time, affecting the appliance's performance. It's essential to clean these components regularly to maintain optimal airflow and heating efficiency. Refer to the manufacturer's instructions for specific guidance on cleaning these internal components safely.

The Ninja Foodi MAX Dual Zone Air Fryer may also come with a removable crumb tray located at the bottom of the appliance. This tray collects any crumbs or drippings during cooking, preventing them from building up inside the appliance. Empty the crumb tray after each use and wash it with warm, soapy water to keep it clean and sanitary.

In terms of maintenance, regular cleaning and inspection of the appliance's components can help identify any issues early on and prevent potential malfunctions. Check the seals, hinges, and other moving parts for signs of wear or damage, and replace them if necessary to ensure the appliance functions correctly.

Lastly, always follow the manufacturer's instructions and recommendations for cleaning and maintenance to preserve the warranty and ensure the safety and performance of your Ninja Foodi MAX Dual Zone Air Fryer. By incorporating these cleaning and maintenance practices into your routine, you can enjoy delicious meals cooked with efficiency and peace of mind.

Chapter 1: Breakfasts

Air Fryer Pizza

Prep Time: 10 minutes   Cook Time: 8 minutes   Serves: 2

Ingredients:

- 400g of pizza dough
- 400g of pizza sauce
- 200g of Mozzarella cheese, grated

Directions:

1. Roll out or cut the fresh pizza dough to fit the size of your air fryer basket (leave a little room around the edges)
2. Spread pizza sauce across the pizza dough.
3. Sprinkle on the cheese.
4. Add any additional pizza toppings. You might need to sprinkle some more cheese on top of them to secure them down.
5. Line the air fryer basket with baking paper, or use a silicone liner. Alternatively, you can brush a little olive oil over the basket.
6. Air fry at 180°C for 8 minutes, checking on it at 6 minutes to ensure it isn't crisping too much.

Nutritional Value (Amount per Serving):

Calories: 905; Fat: 22.26; Carb: 122.26; Protein: 53.52

Air Fryer Burger

Prep Time: 5 minutes   Cook Time: 8 minutes   Serves: 2

Ingredients:

- 2 burger patties - fresh or frozen
- 1/2 onion, chopped
- 2 burger baps
- 2 slices of cheese (optional)
- 2 lettuce leaves (optional)
- 1 tomato, sliced

Directions:

1. Lay the burger patties in the air fryer basket. If you want to cook the onion at the same time you can also add these now.
2. Set the air fryer off at 180°C for 8 minutes.
3. At the 4 minute mark, flip the burger over.
4. At the 8-minute mark check whether the burger is cooked through, the juices should run clear.
5. If you want to turn it into a cheeseburger, lay the slices of cheese over each burger. You can also lightly toast the burger baps at the same time by inserting a trivet and laying them on top of it.
6. Air fry for a further minute, or until the cheese has melted and the baps are lightly toasted.

7. Assemble the burgers in the baps with you choice of salad and sauces.

Nutritional Value (Amount per Serving):

Calories: 522; Fat: 34.77; Carb: 11.97; Protein: 39.07

Air Fryer Turkey Breakfast Sausage

Prep Time: 5 minutes   Cook Time: 15 minutes   Serves: 4

Ingredients:

- 450g of ground turkey (light or dark meat)
- 1 tbsp of light brown sugar
- 2 tsp of finely chopped fresh sage leaves
- 3/4 tsp of kosher salt
- 3/4 tsp of smoked paprika
- 1/2 tsp of crushed red pepper flakes
- 1/2 tsp of fennel seeds, crushed
- 1/2 tsp of garlic powder
- Olive oil cooking spray

Directions:

1. In a medium bowl, combine turkey, brown sugar, sage, salt, paprika, red pepper flakes, fennel seeds, and garlic powder with a fork or your hands until evenly combined. Using damp hands, form turkey mixture into 8 thin patties about 3" in diameter and 1/4" thick (the meat will puff up in the air fryer).
2. Grease an air-fryer basket with cooking spray. Working in batches, arrange patties in basket, spacing about 1/4" apart (do not overcrowd). Cook at 240°C, flipping patties halfway through, until golden and crisp, 5 to 8 minutes.

Nutritional Value (Amount per Serving):

Calories: 180; Fat: 9.09; Carb: 2.17; Protein: 22.57

Air Fryer French Toast Sticks

Prep Time: 5 minutes   Cook Time: 35 minutes   Serves: 6

Ingredients:

- 2 large eggs
- 1/3 c. of heavy cream
- 1/3 c. of whole milk
- 3 tbsp of granulated sugar

- 1/4 tsp of ground cinnamon
- 1/2 tsp of pure vanilla extract
- Kosher salt
- 6 thick slices Pullman or other white loaf or brioche, each slice cut into thirds
- Maple syrup

Directions:

1. Beat eggs, cream, milk, sugar, cinnamon, vanilla, and a pinch of salt in a large shallow baking dish. Add bread, turn to coat a few times.
2. Arrange french toast in basket of air fryer, working in batches as necessary to not overcrowd basket. Set air fryer to 240°C and cook until golden, about 12 minutes, tossing halfway through.
3. Serve toast warm, drizzled with maple syrup.

Nutritional Value (Amount per Serving):

Calories: 315; Fat: 13.93; Carb: 11.57; Protein: 36.7

Air Fryer Fried Brown Rice

Prep Time: 5 minutes   Cook Time: 15 minutes   Serves: 2

Ingredients:

- 1 large carrot, peeled, trimmed, and chopped into small pieces (about 3/4 c.)
- 2 spring onions, thinly sliced, white and green parts separated
- 2 tsp of finely chopped fresh ginger (from a 1" piece)
- 1 tbsp of vegetable oil
- 1/4 tsp of kosher salt
- 2 c. of long-grain brown rice
- 1 clove of garlic, finely chopped
- 2 1/2 tsp of low-sodium soy sauce
- 2 tsp of toasted sesame oil
- Freshly ground black pepper
- 1 large egg, lightly beaten
- 1/2 c. of frozen peas, thawed

Directions:

1. In a 7" nonstick round pan, combine carrot, white parts of spring onions, ginger, vegetable oil, and salt. In an air-fryer basket, place pan. Cook at 200°C, stirring halfway through, until onion and carrot are just tender, about 5 minutes.
2. Remove air-fryer basket and add rice, garlic, soy sauce, sesame oil, and a few grinds of pepper to carrot mixture; stir to combine. Continue to cook at 200°C, until rice is lightly toasted, about 5 minutes more.

3. Remove air-fryer basket and pour egg over half of rice mixture and peas over other half. Continue to cook at 200°C until egg is just set and peas are warm, about 4 minutes more; stir to combine. Top with green parts of spring onions.

Nutritional Value (Amount per Serving):

Calories: 875; Fat: 22.04; Carb: 147.93; Protein: 20.86

Air Fryer Cinnamon Crunch Granola

Prep Time: 5 minutes   Cook Time: 20 minutes   Serves: 4

Ingredients:

- 1/3 c. of packed light brown sugar
- 1/4 c. of extra-virgin olive oil
- 1 tbsp of ground cinnamon
- 2 tsp of pure vanilla extract
- 1/4 tsp of kosher salt
- 1 and a half c. of old-fashioned rolled oats
- 1/2 c. of raw pecans, roughly chopped
- 1/2 c. of raw pumpkin seeds (pepitas)
- 1/2 c. of unsweetened coconut flakes
- 1/4 c. of raw sunflower seeds
- Fresh berries and yogurt, for serving (optional)

Directions:

1. In a large bowl, combine brown sugar, oil, cinnamon, vanilla, and salt. Add oats, pecans, pumpkin seeds, coconut, and sunflower seeds and toss to combine.
2. Line an air-fryer basket with foil, coming 1" up the sides to create a foil basket. Add one-third to one-half of oat mixture (depending on size of air fryer). Cook at 200°C, stirring halfway through, until golden and crispy, 10 to 12 minutes.
3. Transfer to a large heatproof bowl and let cool. Repeat with remaining oat mixture.
4. Serve with berries and yogurt, if desired.
5. Make ahead: Granola can be made 1 month ahead. Store in an airtight container at room temperature.

Nutritional Value (Amount per Serving):

Calories: 345; Fat: 24.5; Carb: 27.83; Protein: 13.93

Air Fryer Cauliflower Tacos

Prep Time: 25 minutes   Cook Time: 45 minutes   Serves: 4

Ingredients:

- 1 c. of thinly sliced red cabbage
- 1/2 small red onion, diced
- 1 jalapeño, minced
- 1 clove of garlic, minced
- Juice of 1 lime
- 2 tbsp of apple cider vinegar
- 1 and a half c. of all-purpose flour
- 1 tsp of chili powder
- 1 tsp of cumin
- 1/2 tsp of garlic powder
- 1/2 tsp of cayenne pepper
- Kosher salt
- Freshly ground black pepper
- 1 1/2 c. of almond milk or other non-dairy milk
- 1 1/2 c. of panko bread crumbs
- 1 medium head cauliflower, cut into bite-size florets
- Cooking spray
- 1/2 c. of vegan mayonnaise
- 2 tbsp of sriracha
- 1 tsp of maple syrup
- Corn tortillas
- Sliced avocado
- Freshly chopped cilantro
- Lime wedges

Directions:

1. In a medium bowl, combine slaw ingredients. Let sit while prepping tacos, stirring every so often.
2. In a medium bowl, combine flour and spices and season well with salt and pepper. Add almond milk and stir to combine. Mixture should be thick, but still easy to dip cauliflower into. Add a little more milk if needed. Place panko into small bowl.
3. Dip florets into milk mixture, wiping any excess off, then toss in panko.
4. Working in batches, place coated cauliflower into basket of air fryer and spray with cooking spray. Cook at 200°C for 15 minutes, stopping about halfway through to toss and spray with more cooking spray.
5. In a small bowl, combine vegan mayonnaise, sriracha, and maple syrup.
6. Assemble tacos: On a tortilla top with cooked cauliflower, avocado, pickled slaw, cilantro, and a drizzle of sriracha mayo. Serve with lime wedges.

Nutritional Value (Amount per Serving):

Calories: 679; Fat: 31.7; Carb: 76.67; Protein: 25.76

Air Fryer Egg Rolls

Prep Time: 10 minutes   Cook Time: 30 minutes   Serves: 12-14

Ingredients:

- Kosher salt

- 1/2 small head of cabbage, cored and thinly sliced
- 2 medium carrots, julienned
- 2 stalks celery, julienned
- Ice
- 3 tbsp of low-sodium soy sauce
- 2 tbsp of hoisin
- 2 tbsp of oyster sauce
- 2 tsp of toasted sesame oil
- 1 tbsp of vegetable or other neutral oil
- 2 cloves of garlic, minced
- 1 tsp of minced fresh ginger
- 450g of pork mince
- Freshly ground black pepper
- 12 to 14 egg roll wrappers
- Hot Chinese mustard and duck sauce

Directions:

1. In a large pot, bring 4 quarts salted water to a boil. Add cabbage, carrots, and celery and cook until slightly softened, about 2 minutes. Transfer to an ice bath.
2. Once cool enough to handle, drain and squeeze veggies with a kitchen towel until water is removed; set aside.
3. In a small bowl, combine soy sauce, hoisin, oyster sauce, and sesame oil.
4. In a large skillet over medium-high heat, heat vegetable oil until shimmering. Cook garlic and ginger, stirring, until fragrant, about 30 seconds. Add pork and cook, breaking up with a spoon, until browned and starting to crisp, 4 to 5 minutes.
5. Drain fat from skillet until about 1 tablespoon remains. Add soy sauce mixture and toss pork to coat. Cook over medium-high heat, stirring, 1 minute. Add veggies and cook, stirring, until combined and warmed through, 2 to 3 minutes more; season with salt and black pepper. Let cool slightly.
6. On a clean work surface, arrange an egg roll wrapper in a diamond shape. Spoon 2 heaping tablespoons filling onto bottom third of wrapper. Fold up bottom half and tightly fold in sides. Gently roll and seal edges with a couple drops of water, pressing to adhere.
7. Working in batches, generously brush egg rolls with vegetable oil. In an air- fryer basket, arrange egg rolls in a single layer. Cook at 240°C, flipping halfway through, until golden brown and crispy, about 10 minutes.
8. Serve egg rolls with mustard and duck sauce alongside.

Nutritional Value (Amount per Serving):

Calories: 276; Fat: 14.2; Carb: 20.49; Protein: 15.74

Air Fryer Oat Pancakes

Prep Time: 5 minutes   Cook Time: 15 minutes   Serves: 1-2

Ingredients:

- 3/4 c. of oat flour
- 3/4 tsp of baking powder
- 1/4 tsp of kosher salt
- 1 large egg
- 1/2 c. of whole milk
- 1 tbsp of butter, melted
- 1 tsp of maple syrup
- 1/2 tsp of pure vanilla extract
- Olive oil cooking spray
- Greek yogurt and fresh fruit

Directions:

1. In a medium bowl, whisk flour, baking powder, and salt. In another medium bowl, whisk egg, milk, butter, syrup, and vanilla. Fold dry ingredients into egg mixture until just combined.
2. In another medium bowl, whisk milk, egg, butter, maple syrup, and vanilla. Fold dry ingredients into wet ingredients until just combined.
3. Grease a 6" pie dish with cooking spray, then add one-quarter (about 1/4 cup) of batter. Place dish in an air-fryer basket. Cook at 200°C until pancake is puffed and lightly golden, about 5 minutes. Repeat with remaining batter.
4. Top pancakes with yogurt, more syrup, and sliced fruit.

Nutritional Value (Amount per Serving):

Calories: 592; Fat: 27.49; Carb: 65.13; Protein: 21.4

Air Fryer Hash Browns

Prep Time: 5 minutes   Cook Time: 25 minutes   Serves: 3-4

Ingredients:

- 3 c. of peeled and grated potatoes, preferably russet
- 1/4 c. of water
- 1 tbsp of vegetable oil
- 3/4 tsp of salt

Directions:

1. In a medium bowl toss together potatoes and water until the potato is fully coated. Cover with plastic wrap and pierce the plastic with a fork a few times.
2. Transfer to the microwave and cook, pausing to toss the mixture every minute, until the potatoes have almost cooked through but still retain bite, and the mixture has grown starchy and slightly sticky, 3 ½ to 4 minutes.
3. Allow potatoes to cool and then toss with oil and salt. Once ready to

handle, form the hash browns into 6 rectangular pucks with rounded edges that are about ¼" thick.

4. Set air fryer to 240°C and cook until the hash browns are golden brown and crispy, 15 to 20 minutes.

Nutritional Value (Amount per Serving):

Calories: 158; Fat: 4.65; Carb: 27.11; Protein: 3.21

Air Fryer Ravioli

Prep Time: 5 minutes   Cook Time: 40 minutes   Serves: 4-6

Ingredients:

- 2 large eggs
- 2 tbsp of whole milk
- 1 c. of Italian bread crumbs
- 1/4 c. of grated Parmesan
- 1/4 tsp of kosher salt
- Freshly ground black pepper
- 1 package (560g) of refrigerated ravioli
- Cooking spray
- Pesto or marinara

Directions:

1. In a shallow bowl, whisk eggs and milk. In another shallow bowl, combine bread crumbs and Parmesan; season with salt and a few grinds of pepper.
2. Working one at a time, dip ravioli into egg mixture, then into bread crumb mixture, pressing to adhere. Dip back into egg mixture. Place on a plate.
3. Lightly coat an air-fryer basket with cooking spray. Working in batches, arrange ravioli in basket, spacing about 1/4" apart; spray with cooking spray. Cook at 240°C, flipping halfway through and spraying with cooking spray, until golden and cooked through, about 7 minutes.
4. Arrange ravioli on a platter. Top with more Parmesan. Serve warm with pesto alongside for dipping.

Nutritional Value (Amount per Serving):

Calories: 193; Fat: 9.43; Carb: 19.21; Protein: 7.71

Air Fryer Chimichanga

Prep Time: 15 minutes   Cook Time: 40 minutes   Serves: 8

Ingredients:

- 1 tbsp of extra-virgin olive oil
- 1 small yellow onion, chopped
- 2 cloves of garlic, minced
- 1 tsp of chili powder
- 1 tsp of ground cumin
- 1/2 tsp of garlic powder
- 3/4 c. of salsa
- 4 c. of shredded cooked chicken

- Kosher salt
- Freshly ground black pepper
- 1 can (425g) of refried beans
- 8 large flour tortillas
- 1 c. of shredded cheddar
- 1 c. of shredded pepper jack
- 1/2 c. of sour cream
- Olive oil cooking spray
- Hot sauce and guacamole

Directions:

1. In a medium skillet over medium heat, heat oil. Cook onion, stirring occasionally, until softened, about 5 minutes. Add garlic, chili powder, cumin, and garlic powder. Cook, stirring, until fragrant, about 1 minute. Add salsa and bring to a simmer, then add chicken and toss to coat; season with salt and black pepper. Remove from heat.
2. Spread about 1/4 cup beans in center of tortillas, then sprinkle with both cheeses. Top with about ½ c. chicken mixture and sour cream. Roll into a burrito by folding top and bottom of tortilla into center, then fold right side over filling, tucking and tightly rolling to seal. Transfer to a plate seam side down.
3. Working in batches, in an air-fryer basket, arrange burritos seam side down; spray with cooking spray. Cook at 200°C for 10 minutes, then turn, spray with more cooking spray, and cook 5 minutes more.
4. Divide chimichangas among plates. Drizzle with hot sauce and sour cream. Serve with guacamole alongside.

Nutritional Value (Amount per Serving):

Calories: 369; Fat: 13.64; Carb: 29.01; Protein: 31.42

Air Fryer Potstickers

Prep Time: 10 minutes   Cook Time: 1 hour   Serves: 25-30

Ingredients:

- 1 c. of Napa cabbage, finely chopped
- Kosher salt
- 120g of sliced bacon, placed in freezer 10 minutes
- 240g of ground chicken
- 3 spring onions, thinly sliced
- 1 piece of ginger, minced
- 1 clove of garlic, minced
- 1 tsp of fish sauce
- 1 tbsp of low-sodium soy sauce
- 1/2 tsp of cornstarch
- 1/2 tsp of white pepper
- 1/4 tsp of toasted sesame oil
- A pinch of granulated sugar
- 25 to 30 dumpling wrappers
- Vegetable oil, for brushing
- Sliced spring onions and dipping sauce, for serving

Directions:

1. Place cabbage in a strainer, season with a good pinch of salt, and toss to combine. Let drain over a bowl about 10 minutes.

2. Meanwhile, chop bacon as fine as you can: Run your knife over bacon until it almost resembles ground meat, about 2 minutes.
3. In a large bowl, combine bacon and chicken. Knead with your hands until mixture turns into a smooth paste, 1 to 2 minutes.
4. Squeeze cabbage of any excess moisture. Add to chicken mixture, along with spring onions, ginger, garlic, fish sauce, soy sauce, cornstarch, white pepper, sesame oil, granulated sugar, and a pinch of salt. Mix with your hands until thoroughly combined, then refrigerate until chilled, about 10 minutes.
5. Place about 2 teaspoons filling in center of a dumpling wrapper. Dip your finger in a bit of water, then run your finger around outside of wrapper. Close dumpling and press 2 sides together into a half moon. Pleat edges to seal, then arrange on a parchment-lined baking sheet. Repeat with remaining wrappers and filling. Cover with a slightly moist kitchen towel until ready to cook.
6. Set the air fryer to 240°C. Working in batches, brush dumplings with vegetable oil. Cook, turning halfway through, until exterior of dumpling is crispy and an instant-read thermometer inserted into center registers 170°, 10 to 12 minutes.
7. Transfer dumplings to a platter. Garnish with spring onions. Serve with desired dipping sauce alongside.
8. Make Ahead: Dumplings can be made 2 months ahead. Cover with plastic and freeze, then transfer to a resealable bag and keep frozen. Place frozen dumplings directly into air fryer. Cook 5 minutes, then brush with oil and return to air fryer. Continue to cook, flipping halfway through, 10 to 12 more minutes.

Nutritional Value (Amount per Serving):

Calories: 53; Fat: 3.89; Carb: 1.83; Protein: 2.86

Air Fryer Flapjacks

Prep Time: 10 minutes   Cook Time: 20 minutes   Serves: 1

Ingredients:

- 250g of butter
- 200g of soft brown sugar
- 4 tbsp of golden syrup
- 400g of porridge oats

Directions:

1. Grease a 20cm square tin and set your air fryer at 160°C.
2. In a saucepan melt the butter and stir in the sugar.
3. Turn off the heat and stir in the oats and golden syrup. Give it a good stir until everything's well mixed.

4. Transfer the flapjack mixture into the greased tin. Use the back of a spoon or a palette knife to press it down until it's nice and compact.
5. Transfer the tin to the air fryer basket and set the timer for 20 minutes. Check on it after around 15 minutes. When it is ready, the mixture will be slightly firm to the touch but still slightly runny. The flapjacks will become too hard and tough to eat if you leave the edges and top to turn a darker golden brown.
6. Remove the tin from the air fryer basket and leave the flapjacks to cool down. Don't try to take them out beforehand or they might crumble.
7. When they have cooled down, slice them up and enjoy!

Nutritional Value (Amount per Serving):

Calories: 3804; Fat: 231.07; Carb: 532.15; Protein: 71.33

Air Fryer Hot Dogs

Prep Time: 5 minutes   Cook Time: 10 minutes   Serves: 6

Ingredients:

- 6 hot dogs
- 6 hot dog buns

Directions:

1. Place hot dogs in basket of air fryer. Cook at 200°C for 4 minutes. Remove from basket.
2. Place buns in basket and cook at 200°C for 2 minutes to toast them, if desired.
3. Place hot dogs in buns and top with desired toppings.

Nutritional Value (Amount per Serving):

Calories: 129; Fat: 0.65; Carb: 33.1; Protein: 2.13

Air Fryer Cheeseburgers

Prep Time: 10 minutes   Cook Time: 20 minutes   Serves: 4

Ingredients:

- 450g of beef mince
- 2 cloves of garlic, crushed
- 1 tbsp of low-sodium soy sauce
- Salt
- Freshly ground black pepper
- 4 slices of American cheese
- 4 hamburger buns
- Mayonnaise
- Lettuce
- Sliced tomatoes
- Thinly sliced red onion

Directions:

1. In a large bowl combine beef, garlic, and soy sauce. Shape into 4 patties

and flatten into a 11cm circle. Season both sides with salt and pepper.

2. Place 2 patties in air fryer and cook at 180°C for 4 minutes per side, for medium. Remove and immediately top with a slice of cheese. Repeat with remaining 2 patties.

3. Spread hamburger buns with mayo, then top with lettuce, patties, tomatoes, and onions.

Nutritional Value (Amount per Serving):

Calories: 710; Fat: 38.81 ; Carb: 39.52; Protein: 52.18

Air Fryer Cinnamon Rolls

Prep Time: 5 minutes   Cook Time: 25 minutes   Serves: 6

Ingredients:

- 2 tbsp of melted butter, plus more for brushing
- 75g of packed brown sugar
- 1/2 tsp of ground cinnamon
- Salt
- Plain flour, for surface
- 225g of ready rolled pizza dough
- 50g of cream cheese, softened
- 65g of icing sugar
- 1 tbsp whole milk, plus more if needed

Directions:

1. Make rolls: Line bottom of air fryer with parchment paper and brush with butter. In a medium bowl, combine butter, brown sugar, cinnamon, and a large pinch of salt until smooth and fluffy.

2. On a lightly floured surface, roll out dough in one piece. Pinch seams together and fold in half. Roll into a 22-cm x 18-cm rectangle. Spread butter mixture over dough, leaving 1.5-cm border. Starting at a long edge, roll up dough, then cut crosswise into 6 pieces.

3. Arrange pieces in prepared air fryer, cut-side up, spaced evenly.

4. Set air fryer to 180°C, and cook until golden and cooked through, about 10 minutes.

5. Make the glaze: In a medium bowl, Whisk cream cheese, icing sugar, and milk together. Add more milk by the teaspoonful, if necessary, to thin glaze.

6. Spread glaze over warm cinnamon rolls and serve.

Nutritional Value (Amount per Serving):

Calories: 285; Fat: 8.54; Carb: 45.86; Protein: 6.34

Air Fryer Fry-up

Prep Time: 15 minutes   Cook Time: 30 minutes   Serves: 1

Ingredients:

- 1 English muffin
- 1/2 tsp of butter, softened
- 200g of mushrooms, roughly chopped
- 1/2 tsp of olive oil
- 1 tomato, halved across the equator
- 2 sausages
- 2 hash browns
- 1 egg
- 2 bacon rashers
- 200g can baked beans (optional)

Directions:

1. Set the air-fryer to 180°C. Slice the English muffin in half and cut a circle out of one half, leaving a 2cm-thick ring. Toast for 5-6 mins in the air-fryer, remove, then butter the whole half and press the other half onto it. Set aside.
2. Put the mushrooms in a bowl and drizzle over the oil. Season with salt and pepper and stir to coat. Tip the mushrooms into the air-fryer and cook for 4 mins until beginning to soften. Season the cut halves of the tomato, then put in the air-fryer with the mushrooms and add the sausages, too. Cook for 2 mins before adding the hash browns and cook for another 4 mins.
3. Meanwhile, crack the egg into a small cup or ramekin. Put the muffin on a plate, then pour the egg into the hole on top of the muffin. Set aside.
4. At this point your air-fryer is likely to be quite full, so spoon the mushrooms on top of the tomatoes to make some room. Put the bacon on top of the sausages, then carefully nestle in the egg muffin. Cook for 8-10 mins. If your air-fryer is large enough, pour the beans into a ramekin and nestle in to cook as well. Alternatively, microwave the beans for 2 mins to heat through.

Nutritional Value (Amount per Serving):

Calories: 1434; Fat: 50; Carb: 230.42; Protein: 52.97

Air Fryer Cheese & Ham Toastie

Prep Time: 10 minutes   Cook Time: 10 minutes   Serves: 1

Ingredients:

- 20g of butter, softened
- 2 slices of sourdough bread or other bread
- 1/2 tsp of English mustard
- 50g of grated mature cheddar or gruyère

- 1 tbsp of chopped chives (optional)
- 1 thick slice of ham

Directions:

1. Set the air-fryer to 190°C. Butter the slices of bread on one side each, then combine the remaining butter with the mustard, cheese and chives, if using. Season with black pepper.
2. Spread the cheese mixture over the plain sides of the bread, then sandwich the ham between the two slices so the buttered sides are facing out. Air-fry for 10 mins, turning once until golden and crunchy on the outside, and the cheese has melted in the middle.

Nutritional Value (Amount per Serving):

Calories: 486; Fat: 32.36; Carb: 27.23; Protein: 22

Air Fryer Boiled Eggs

Prep Time: 1 minute   Cook Time: 10 minutes   Serves: 1

Ingredients:

- 4 eggs (cook as many as you need)

Directions:

1. Add room temperature eggs to the basket of your air fryer, and leave some space between them so that there is room for the hot air to circulate. Use a metal rack if needed to fit more in.
2. Set the air fryer temperature at 150°C. Cook according to how well done you want your eggs (starting at 8 minutes for runny, up to 12 minutes for hard boiled).
3. At the end of the cooking time remove from the air fryer basket and plunge into an ice bath or into a bowl of cold water – this will prevent the eggs from continuing to cook.
4. Once they have cooled down a little and can be handled, remove the shell.

Nutritional Value (Amount per Serving):

Calories: 518; Fat: 38.56; Carb: 4.06; Protein: 35.87

Chapter 2: Meat Recipes

Beef Nachos

Prep Time: 20 minutes   Cook Time: 20 minutes   Serves: 6

Ingredients:

- 1-2 tsp of chilli flakes
- 1 tsp of ground coriander
- 1 tsp of ground cumin
- 1 tbsp of vegetable oil
- 500g of beef mince
- 2 tbsp of tomato purée
- 2 garlic cloves
- 300ml of water
- 200g of tinned black beans
- ½ lime
- 1 bunch of fresh coriander
- Monterey Jack cheese
- Chopped avocado

Directions:

1. In a dry pan, toast the chilli flakes, coriander and cumin for 1 minute. Remove.
2. Heat the vegetable oil in the pan and brown the beef mince.
3. Stir in the tomato purée, garlic and the toasted spices, then cook for 2 minutes. Pour over the water and simmer for 10 minutes.
4. Add the black beans, drained and rinsed, and cook for 5 minutes. Add the lime juice and coriander leaves. Build the nachos in lined air fryer basket (or in a heatproof dish) in the air fryer and cook for 5 mins at 180°C.

Nutritional Value (Amount per Serving):

Calories: 344; Fat: 15.57; Carb: 25.72; Protein: 27.8

Air Fryer Meatballs With Crispy Potatoes

Prep Time: 15 minutes   Cook Time: 20 minutes   Serves: 2

Ingredients:

- 2 medium floury potatoes, cut into 1.5cm chunks
- 3 tsp of olive oil
- 2 garlic cloves, finely chopped
- 1 small red chilli, finely chopped
- 200g of cherry tomatoes, halved
- 500g of passata
- 1 tsp of red wine vinegar
- 12 British beef meatballs
- 2 tbsp of black olive tapenade
- Chopped parsley

Directions:

1. Set the air fryer to 200°C. Coat the potatoes in 2 tsp of the oil, then put

them in the air fryer basket, ideally in a single layer. Cook for 10 minutes.

2. Meanwhile, heat the remaining olive oil in a small saucepan over a low-medium heat. Add the garlic and chilli, cook gently for 1 minutes, then add the cherry tomatoes. Cook for a few minutes until they begin to break down, then stir in the passata and simmer for 5-6 minutes until reduced a little. Season with the vinegar and a pinch of salt and pepper.

3. Coat the meatballs in the tapenade. After they've been cooking for 10 minutes, give the potatoes a shake, then put the meatballs on top. Air-fry both the meatballs and potatoes for a further 10 minutes, until the potatoes are crisp and the meatballs have browned. Serve the meatballs covered in the tomato sauce with a scattering of parsley and the potatoes alongside.

Nutritional Value (Amount per Serving):

Calories: 596; Fat: 14.92; Carb: 87.21; Protein: 33.05

Air Fryer Sausage and Pepper Stew

Prep Time: 10 minutes   Cook Time: 28 minutes   Serves: 2

Ingredients:

- 2 onions, cut into wedges
- 2 red or yellow peppers, sliced
- 100g of cherry tomatoes
- 3 tbsp of olive oil
- 6 sausages
- 1 tsp of fennel seeds
- 1 and a half tsp of smoked paprika
- 100ml of white wine

Directions:

1. Set the air fryer to 200°C and remove the grill rack if it has one. Put the onions, peppers and tomatoes in the air fryer, drizzle with the oil and season with salt and pepper, then cook for 10 minutes.

2. Add the sausages, fennel seeds and paprika, stir well, then cook for 10 more minutes.

3. Turn the sausages, pour in the wine then turn the heat down to 180°C. Cook for a final 8 minutes until the vegetables are tender and the sausages are browned all over.

Nutritional Value (Amount per Serving):

Calories: 501; Fat: 36.29; Carb: 32.6; Protein: 18.97

Air Fryer Korean-Inspired Pork Tenderloin Lettuce Wraps

Prep Time: 5 minutes   Cook Time: 25 minutes   Serves: 2-4

Ingredients:

- 450g of pork tenderloin
- 3/4 tsp of kosher salt
- 1/4 c. of gochujang (Korean hot pepper paste)
- 1 clove of garlic, finely grated
- 2 tbsp of honey
- 1 tbsp of toasted sesame oil
- 1/4 tsp of finely grated fresh ginger
- 1 tbsp of unseasoned rice vinegar
- Olive oil cooking spray
- 1 head of Bibb or butter lettuce, leaves separated
- Sliced cucumber, sliced spring onions, and cooked rice

Directions:

1. Cut pork in half crosswise; season all over with salt.
2. In a medium bowl, combine gochujang, garlic, honey, oil, and ginger. Transfer 1/4 cup gochujang mixture to a small bowl and stir in vinegar; set aside for serving. Add pork to bowl with remaining sauce and toss to coat.
3. Lightly coat an air-fryer basket with cooking spray. Place pork in basket and cook at 220°C, turning occasionally, until pork is golden brown and an instant- read thermometer inserted into thickest part registers 140°C, 16 to 19 minutes. Let rest about 10 minutes before slicing.
4. Place pork in lettuce leaves, along with cucumber, scallions, and rice. Serve with reserved sauce alongside.

Nutritional Value (Amount per Serving):

Calories: 509; Fat: 32.92; Carb: 13.21; Protein: 39.87

Air Fryer Steak Bites

Prep Time: 10 minutes   Cook Time: 20minutes   Serves: 4

Ingredients:

- 450g of New York strip steak, trimmed and cut into 1" cubes
- 1 tbsp of Worcestershire sauce
- 1/2 tsp of freshly ground black pepper
- 2 and a half tsp of kosher salt, divided
- 1/2 c. (1 stick) of unsalted butter, divided
- 6 cloves of garlic, finely chopped
- 2 tsp (or more) of finely chopped fresh parsley

Directions:

1. Set air fryer at 220°C. Meanwhile, in a large bowl, toss steak,

Worcestershire sauce, pepper, and 2 teaspoons salt.

2. Working in batches if necessary, arrange steak in air fryer basket in a single layer. Cook 2 minutes, then flip and continue to cook until medium-rare, 1 to 2 minutes more, or to desired degree of doneness. Transfer steak to a plate and keep warm.

3. Meanwhile, in a small pot over medium heat, melt 2 tablespoons butter. Stir in garlic and remaining 1/2 teaspoon salt and cook, stirring occasionally, until sizzling and fragrant, about 1 minute. Add remaining 6 tablespoons butter and stir until melted, about 1 minute more. Remove from heat and stir in parsley.

4. Drizzle steak with half of garlic butter. Top with more parsley, if desired. Serve with remaining garlic butter alongside for dipping.

Nutritional Value (Amount per Serving):

Calories: 292; Fat: 19.22; Carb: 2.35; Protein: 28.09

Lamb Chapli Kebabs

Prep Time: 15 minutes   Cook Time: 10 minutes   Serves: 4

Ingredients:

- 500g of lamb mince
- 1 medium onion, finely diced and excess moisture squeezed out
- 1 medium tomato, deseeded and finely diced
- 1 green chilli, finely diced
- 1 and a quarter tsp of coriander powder
- 1 tsp of cumin powder
- 7.5g of salt
- 1 and a half tsp of chilli flakes
- 1/2 tsp of garam masala
- 1 and a half tbsp of flour/besan or plain flour

Directions:

1. Start by ensuring that the diced onions have had their excess moisture removed as moisture can interfere with the kebab's texture.

2. In a mixing bowl, combine the lamb mince, onions, tomatoes and fresh chillies.

3. Add all the spices and the gram or plain flour to the mixture.

4. Mix thoroughly until the ingredients are well combined and the mixture becomes sticky, clinging to your hands.

5. Divide the mixture into six equal portions and shape each into a patty. As an optional addition, you can insert a slice of tomato into each kebab.

6. Brush or spray the patties with oil, then air fry at 180°C for 8 minutes.

Nutritional Value (Amount per Serving):

Calories: 351; Fat: 21.44; Carb: 6.4; Protein: 31.73

Air Fryer Beef Empanadas

Prep Time: 20 minutes   Cook Time: 1 hour 40 minutes   Serves: 1

Ingredients:

- 360 g of all-purpose flour
- 1 tsp of kosher salt
- 1 tsp of baking powder
- 1/2 c. (1 stick) of cold unsalted butter, cut into cubes
- 1 large egg
- 1 tbsp of extra-virgin olive oil
- 1 yellow onion, chopped
- 2 cloves of garlic, finely chopped
- 450g beef mince
- 1 tbsp of tomato paste
- 1 tsp of dried oregano
- 1 tsp of ground cumin
- 1/2 tsp of paprika
- Kosher salt
- Freshly ground black pepper
- 1/2 c. of chopped pickled jalapeños
- 1/2 c. of chopped tomatoes
- 1 and a quarter c. of shredded cheddar
- 1 and a quarter c. of shredded Monterey Jack
- Chopped fresh cilantro and sour cream

Directions:

1. In a large bowl, whisk flour, salt, and baking powder. Cut butter into flour with your hands or a pastry cutter until pea-sized pieces form. Add egg and 3/4 cup water and mix with a wooden spoon until a dough forms.
2. Turn out dough on a lightly floured surface and knead until smooth, about 5 minutes.
3. Wrap dough in plastic wrap and refrigerate at least 1 hour or up to overnight.
4. In a large skillet over medium heat, heat oil. Add onion and cook, stirring occasionally, until softened, about 7 minutes. Add garlic and cook, stirring, until fragrant, about 1 minute more. Add beef and cook, breaking meat up with a wooden spoon, until no longer pink, about 5 minutes. Drain fat.
5. Return pan to medium heat and stir tomato paste into beef mixture. Add

oregano, cumin, and paprika; season with salt and pepper. Add jalapeños and tomatoes and cook, stirring, until warmed through, about 3 minutes. Let cool slightly.

6. On a lightly floured surface, divide dough in half. Roll one half to 1/4" thick. Using a 4.5" round cookie cutter, cut out rounds. Repeat with remaining dough. Reroll scraps once to cut out more rounds (you should have about 15).

7. Lightly moisten outer edge of a dough round with water. Place about 2 tablespoons filling in the center. Top with some cheddar and Monterey. Fold dough in half over filling. Using a fork, crimp edges together. Repeat with remaining filling, dough, and cheese.

8. Set air fryer to 240°C. Working in batches, arrange empanadas in a parchment-lined air fryer basket, making sure they don't touch.

9. Cook empanadas until golden brown and filling is warmed through, about 15 minutes.

10. Top with cilantro and serve with sour cream alongside.

Nutritional Value (Amount per Serving):

Calories: 4016; Fat: 226.02; Carb: 330.1; Protein: 169.96

Air-Fryer Pork Chops

Prep Time: 5 minutes   Cook Time: 12 minutes   Serves: 4

Ingredients:

- 4 pork ribs
- 1/2 tbsp of sunflower or vegetable oil
- 1/2 tsp of dried oregano
- 1/2 tsp of paprika
- 1/2 tsp of mustard powder
- 1/2 tsp of onion powder
- 25g of parmesan, finely grated
- cooked greens and peas, to serve (optional)

Directions:

1. Set the air-fryer to 190°C. Put the pork chops in a bowl, drizzle over the oil and rub all over the chops.

2. Combine the oregano, paprika, mustard powder, onion powder and parmesan with 1/2 tsp of salt and 1/2 tsp of freshly ground black pepper. Sprinkle over the pork chops, ensuring they are covered.

3. Put the chops in the air-fryer basket and cook for 5 mins. Turn over, then cook for 5-8 mins more until cooked through. Timings will depend on the thickness and whether they're bone-in or not. A temperature probe should

read 75°C in the thickest part of the chop. Serve with wilted greens and peas, if you like.

Nutritional Value (Amount per Serving):

Calories: 326; Fat: 13.3; Carb: 4.63; Protein: 44.14

Air-Fryer Beef Joint

Prep Time: 5 minutes   Cook Time: 40 minutes   Serves: 6-8

Ingredients:

- 1.2kg of beef joint
- 1-2 tbsp of neutral-flavoured oil
- 1 tsp of dried thyme
- 1 tsp of onion granules
- 1 tsp of mustard powder

Directions:

5. Take the beef out of the fridge and bring it up to room temperature before cooking (20-30 mins should do it).
6. Set the air-fryer at 220°C. Rub the beef all over with the oil, then combine the thyme, onion granules and mustard powder with 1 tsp salt and 1 tsp ground black pepper in a bowl. Rub this all over the beef joint, then put the beef in the air-fryer basket and cook for 10 mins.
7. Reduce the temperature to 170°C, then cook for a further 30-40 mins (30 mins for medium-rare and 40 mins for medium-well done). Transfer the meat to a board, cover loosely with foil, and leave to rest for up to 30 mins before carving and serving.

Nutritional Value (Amount per Serving):

Calories: 269; Fat: 12.77; Carb: 3.64; Protein: 35.59

Air Fryer Meatloaf

Prep Time: 15 minutes   Cook Time: 1 hour   Serves: 4

Ingredients:

- 450g lean beef mince
- 1/2 yellow onion, finely chopped
- 1/2 green bell pepper, finely chopped
- 1 large egg
- 1/2 c. of plain bread crumbs
- 1 tsp of kosher salt
- 1 tsp of freshly ground black pepper
- 1/4 c. plus 2 tbsp of ketchup, divided
- 9 strips of bacon, halved
- 2 tbsp of brown sugar

Directions:

1. Set an air fryer to 240°C. In a large bowl, combine beef, onion, bell pepper, egg, bread crumbs, salt, black pepper, and 2 tbsp of ketchup. Using your

hands, mix until evenly incorporated.

2. On a piece of parchment paper, form beef mixture into 2 equal loaves that will fit in your air fryer. Layer bacon slices on top of loaves.

3. In a small bowl, whisk brown sugar and remaining 1/4 c. of ketchup. Brush onto bacon.

4. Place pan on a rimmed baking sheet or something similar that fits your air fryer, as juices may overflow during baking. Bake, tenting with foil if bacon starts to burn, until an instant-read thermometer inserted in center of loaves registers 160° and top is golden brown, 25 to 30 minutes.

5. Make Ahead: Meatloaf can be made 3 days ahead. Transfer to an airtight container and chill.

Nutritional Value (Amount per Serving):

Calories: 350; Fat: 14.26; Carb: 27.56; Protein: 28.84

Air-Fryer Gammon

Prep Time: 5 minutes   Cook Time: 1 hour   Serves: 10

Ingredients:

- 1 unsmoked gammon joint (around 750g)
- 2 tbsp of Dijon mustard
- 2 tbsp of honey or maple syrup
- sliced bread, butter and pineapple salsa (optional, see right), to serve

Directions:

1. Remove the gammon from the fridge around 45 mins before you want to start the recipe. Combine the mustard and honey or syrup in a small bowl and season with salt and freshly ground black pepper. Brush this all over the gammon, reserving any leftover glaze, and wrap the gammon in foil.

2. Set the air-fryer at 160°C. Put the gammon in the air-fryer and cook for 1 hr, brushing with more glaze every 20 mins if you can. The gammon should be cooked through (use a digital thermometer to check – it should read 70°C). Remove and leave to rest for 10-15 mins before carving. (To recycle the foil, make sure you scrunch it into a ball before placing in household recycling.)

3. If you're making a sandwich, carve a few slices of gammon. Butter the bread, then top one slice with 1-2 tbsp of pineapple salsa, layer on the slices of gammon and top with another slice of bread.

Nutritional Value (Amount per Serving):

Calories: 18; Fat: 0.17; Carb: 3.85; Protein: 0.29

Air Fryer Crispy Chilli Beef

Prep Time: 15 minutes   Cook Time: 15 minutes   Serves: 2

Ingredients:

- 250g of thin-cut minute steak, thinly sliced into strips
- 2 tbsp of cornflour
- 2 tbsp of vegetable oil, plus a drizzle
- 2 garlic cloves, crushed
- thumb-sized piece of ginger, peeled and cut into matchsticks
- 1 red chilli, thinly sliced
- 1 red pepper, cut into chunks
- 4 spring onions, sliced, green and white parts separated
- 4 tbsp of rice wine vinegar or white wine vinegar
- 1 tbsp of soy sauce
- 2 tbsp of sweet chilli sauce
- 2 tbsp of tomato ketchup
- 1/2 tsp of Chinese five-spice powder
- 2 tsp of soy sauce
- 1 tsp of sesame oil
- 1 tsp of caster sugar

Directions:

1. First, combine the marinade ingredients in a bowl. Add the steak strips and toss to coat. Leave in the fridge for up to 24 hrs if you can, or carry on to step 2.
2. Sprinkle the cornflour over the steak and mix until each piece is coated in a floury paste. Pull the strips apart and arrange over a plate. Drizzle each piece of steak with a little oil. Set the air fryer to 220°C.
3. Carefully put the beef on the cooking rack in the air fryer, cook for 6 mins, thenturn and cook for another 4-6 mins until crispy.
4. Meanwhile, heat 2 tbsp of vegetable oil in a wok over a high heat and stir-fry the garlic, ginger, chilli, pepper and white ends of the spring onions for 2-3 mins until the pepper softens. Be careful not to burn the ginger and garlic. Add the vinegar, soy, sweet chilli sauce and tomato ketchup, mix well and cook for another minute until bubbling.
5. Tip the beef into the wok and toss through the sauce. Continue cooking for another minute until piping hot, then serve scattered with the spring onion greens and a little extra sauce on the side.

Nutritional Value (Amount per Serving):

Calories: 658; Fat: 56.18; Carb: 14.08; Protein: 25.96

Air fryer steak

Prep Time: 2 minutes   Cook Time: 10-15 minutes   Serves: 2

Ingredients:

- 2 rib-eye steaks, around 260g of each and 3cm thick
- 1 tsp of oil

Directions:

1. Dry off the steaks using kitchen paper or a clean cloth. Brush with the oil, then season generously with salt and freshly ground black pepper.
2. Set the air fryer for on 200°C. Put the steaks in the basket and cook for 6 mins. Turn the steak and cook for a further 2 mins. At this point, your steak should be rare to medium rare. Cook for a further 2 mins for medium steaks, plus 2 mins more if you prefer them well-done.
3. Remove the steaks and put on a plate to rest for 3-4 mins. This is a perfect opportunity to make a sauce, if you like.

Nutritional Value (Amount per Serving):

Calories: 22; Fat: 2.46 ; Carb: 0; Protein: 0.18

Air Fryer Beef & Broccoli

Prep Time: 10 minutes   Cook Time: 20 minutes   Serves: 2-4

Ingredients:

- 1/2 c. of low-sodium chicken broth
- 3 tbsp of reduced-sodium soy sauce
- 2 tbsp of packed light brown sugar
- 1 tbsp of cornstarch
- 1 tsp of Shaoxing wine or dry sherry
- 1 tsp of toasted sesame oil
- Freshly ground black pepper
- 450g flank or skirt steak, cut against the grain into 1/8" slices, then cut into 1" to 2" pieces
- 2 cloves of garlic, finely chopped
- 1 tbsp of reduced-sodium soy sauce
- 2 tsp of cornstarch
- 2 tsp of finely chopped peeled fresh ginger
- 2 tsp of Shaoxing wine or dry sherry
- 340g small broccoli florets (from about 2 heads)
- 2 tbsp of vegetable oil
- Thinly sliced spring onions, toasted sesame seeds, and steamed or sticky

rice, for serving

Directions:

1. In a medium heatproof bowl, whisk broth, soy sauce, brown sugar, cornstarch, and wine. Microwave on high, stirring halfway through, until sauce is thickened, about 2 minutes. Stir in oil; season with a few grinds of black pepper.
2. In another medium bowl, toss steak with garlic, soy sauce, cornstarch, ginger, and wine. Let sit 5 minutes. Add broccoli and oil and toss to combine.
3. Arrange half of steak and broccoli mixture in a single layer in an air fryer basket. Cook at 240°C until steak is just cooked through and broccoli is tender and golden in spots, 8 to 10 minutes. Scrape cooked steak and broccoli mixture into bowl with sauce.
4. Repeat with remaining steak and broccoli mixture, then toss to coat in sauce.
5. Sprinkle with scallions and sesame seeds. Serve over rice.

Nutritional Value (Amount per Serving):

Calories: 733; Fat: 59.12; Carb: 20.09; Protein: 32.58

Air Fryer Bacon

Prep Time: 1 minute   Cook Time: 10 minutes   Serves: 1

Ingredients:

- 4 bacon rashers

Directions:

1. Lay the bacon rashers in the air fryer basket. If you want to fit more rashers in, either use a trivet or a rack to add more. It doesn't matter if the bacon rashers are touching each other, or if they are overlapping a little bit, but don't lay them on top of each other.
2. Set the air fryer off at 180°C for 8 to 10 minutes. For thicker slices of bacon, increase the time to 12-15 minutes. Flip the bacon halfway through (unless you are using a crisping rack).
3. If the bacon isn't crispy enough, cook it for a little longer, checking on it after 2 minutes.

Nutritional Value (Amount per Serving):

Calories: 264; Fat: 25.12; Carb: 5.38; Protein: 9.09

Air Fryer Meatballs

Prep Time: 5 minutes   Cook Time: 10 minutes   Serves: 1

Ingredients:

- 500g lean beef mince
- 1 clove garlic, crushed
- 1 tsp dried mixed herbs
- 1 egg
- 1tbsp breadcrumbs (optional)

Directions:

1. If you are making meatballs from scratch, mix all the ingredients together until well combined.
2. Using your hands, form small round balls (this recipe makes about 12, depending on size of meatballs)
3. Place the meatballs in air fryer basket and cook at 180°C for 8 to 10 minutes. Check half way through and turn over/shake about.
4. If you want to add a sauce, either make it/heat it on the stove while the meatballs are cooking or alternatively you can heat the sauce in the air fryer with the meatballs. You will need to transfer the cooked meatballs to an ovenproof dish/pan that will fit in the air fryer basket. Pour the meatball sauce on top and place container in the air fryer basket. Cook at 180°C for about 3-4 minutes, or until the sauce is hot.
5. Serve with spaghetti and melted cheese.

Nutritional Value (Amount per Serving):

Calories: 799; Fat: 38.2; Carb: 2.02; Protein: 111.76

Chapter 3: Poultry Recipes

Air fryer chicken breast salad

Prep Time: 10 minutes   Cook Time: 20 minutes   Serves: 2

Ingredients:

- 2 skinless free-range chicken breasts
- Juice of 1 lemon
- 1 tbsp of olive oil
- 1 tbsp of smoked paprika
- 1 tsp of sea salt
- 1 tsp of freshly ground black pepper
- 1 tsp of cayenne pepper
- 1/2 tsp of dried oregano
- 1 tbsp of runny honey
- 1 tbsp of Dijon mustard
- 2 tbsp of extra-virgin olive oil
- 1 tbsp of cider vinegar
- 1 garlic clove, finely grated
- Handful cherry tomatoes, halved
- 1/2 iceberg lettuce, roughly chopped
- 1 tbsp of capers, drained

Directions:

1. Put each chicken breast between 2 sheets of baking paper and bash with a rolling pin until evenly flat all over (they don't have to be super-thin, just the same thickness throughout). Use a fork to prick lots of little holes in the chicken, then put them in a dish and coat with the lemon juice and olive oil.
2. Set the air fryer to 190°C. Mix the paprika, salt, pepper, cayenne and oregano together, then massage the mixture all over the chicken breasts, ensuring an even, liberal coverage. Put the chicken in the air fryer and cook for 16 minutes, turning halfway.
3. While the chicken cooks, put the honey, mustard, oil, vinegar and garlic in a clean jam jar, season with a generous pinch of salt and pepper and shake to create a dressing. Season the tomatoes with a pinch of salt.
4. To serve, toss the lettuce in some of the dressing to coat, then divide between bowls. Arrange the tomatoes and capers on top. Slice the chicken breasts and put them in the centre, then drizzle over the remaining dressing.

Nutritional Value (Amount per Serving):

Calories: 310; Fat: 17.14; Carb: 17.6; Protein: 24.13

Air Fryer Crispy Chicken Sandwich

Prep Time: 10 minutes   Cook Time: 35 minutes   Serves: 4

Ingredients:

- 4 (110g) chicken cutlets
- Kosher salt

- Freshly ground black pepper
- 2 large eggs
- 4 tsp of yellow or honey mustard
- 1 tbsp of bread-and-butter pickle juice
- 1/2 tsp of sweet paprika
- 1/4 tsp of garlic powder
- 1/8 tsp of cayenne
- 1 c. of plain bread crumbs
- 1/4 c. of all-purpose flour
- Olive oil cooking spray
- 4 lightly toasted potato rolls
- Lettuce leaves and sliced tomatoes

Directions:

1. Pat chicken dry with paper towels; season all over with 3/4 teaspoon salt and 1/4 teaspoon of black pepper.
2. In a shallow bowl, whisk eggs, mustard, pickle juice, paprika, garlic powder, and cayenne until combined. Place bread crumbs and flour in separate shallow bowls.
3. Dip one chicken cutlet into flour, shaking off any excess. Dip chicken into egg mixture, letting any excess drip off. Coat chicken in breadcrumbs, gently pressing to adhere. Transfer breaded cutlet to a plate.
4. Generously coat an air-fryer basket with cooking spray. Working in batches, arrange 2 cutlets in a single layer in basket. Generously spray chicken with cooking spray until evenly coated. Cook at 240°C, flipping halfway through and generously spraying second side with cooking spray, until breading is golden brown and chicken is just cooked through, 8 to 10 minutes. Transfer to a wire rack and let cool 5 minutes.
5. Arrange chicken on bottom bun. Layer lettuce, tomato, and pickles over chicken. Spread top bun with mustard and close sandwich.

Nutritional Value (Amount per Serving):

Calories: 1476; Fat: 32.44; Carb: 78.34; Protein: 205.55

Air Fryer Chipotle Chicken Meatballs

Prep Time: 5 minutes   Cook Time: 20 minutes   Serves: 2-4

Ingredients:

- 450g of chicken mince (93% lean)
- 3/4 c. of panko bread crumbs
- 1/4 c. of chopped fresh cilantro
- 1 large egg, beaten
- 3 cloves of garlic, minced
- 1 tbsp of finely chopped chipotle chiles in adobo sauce, plus 2 tsp of sauce
- 3/4 tsp of dried oregano
- 3/4 tsp of kosher salt
- 1/4 tsp of freshly ground black pepper

- Olive oil cooking spray
- Salsa verde

Directions:

1. In a medium bowl, using your hands, mix ground chicken, panko, cilantro, egg, garlic, chipotle chiles and sauce, oregano, salt, and pepper until combined. Roll into 1" balls.
2. Lightly coat an air-fryer basket with cooking spray. Working in batches, arrange meatballs in basket, spacing about 1/2" apart. Cook at 240°C, turning a few times, until outsides of meatballs are golden brown and centers are cooked through, about 6 minutes.
3. Arrange meatballs on a platter. Spoon salsa verde over top or serve alongside for dipping.

Nutritional Value (Amount per Serving):

Calories: 225; Fat: 6.47; Carb: 6.54; Protein: 33.19

Air Fryer Cilantro-Lime Cornish Hen

Prep Time: 5 minutes   Cook Time: 45 minutes   Serves: 1-2

Ingredients:

- 1 whole cornish hen (about 1 1/2 lb.)
- 1/2 tsp of kosher salt
- 1/4 tsp of freshly ground black pepper
- 1 clove of garlic, minced
- 2 tbsp of chopped fresh cilantro
- leaves
- 1 tbsp of extra-virgin olive oil
- 1 tbsp of fresh lime juice
- 3/4 tsp of low-sodium soy sauce
- 1/4 tsp of ground cumin
- Lime wedges

Directions:

1. Pat cornish hen dry with paper towels; season all over with salt and pepper.
2. In a medium bowl, combine garlic, cilantro, oil, lime juice, soy sauce, and cumin. Add cornish hen and toss to coat. Let marinate at least 15 minutes at room temperature, or cover bowl and refrigerate up to 1 hour.
3. Remove cornish hen from marinade. In an air-fryer basket, arrange cornish hen breast side down. Pour any marinade remaining in bowl over top
4. of cornish hen. Cook at 220°C, flipping halfway through, until skin is golden and crisp and cornish hen is just cooked through, 25 to 30 minutes.
5. Transfer cornish hen to a platter. Pour any juices from bottom of air-fryer basket over top. Top with more cilantro. Serve with lime wedges alongside.

Nutritional Value (Amount per Serving):

Calories: 514; Fat: 29.78; Carb: 39.11; Protein: 24.19

Air Fryer Tandoori Turkey Breast

Prep Time: 5 minutes   Cook Time: 1 hour 15 minutes   Serves: 4

Ingredients:

- 1 split skin-on, bone-in turkey breast (about 1 3/4 lb.)
- 1 and a half tsp of kosher salt, divided
- 1 c. of full-fat plain Greek yogurt
- 2 cloves of garlic, minced
- 1 tbsp of sweet paprika
- 2 tsp of ground turmeric
- 2 tsp of minced fresh ginger (from a 1" piece)
- 1 tsp of ground cumin
- Olive oil cooking spray

Directions:

1. Pat turkey dry with paper towels; season all over with 1 teaspoon salt.
2. In a medium bowl, combine yogurt, garlic, paprika, turmeric, ginger, cumin, and remaining 1/2 teaspoon of salt. Spread yogurt mixture all over turkey. Let stand at room temperature for 30 minutes.
3. Lightly coat an air-fryer basket with cooking spray. Place turkey in basket. Cook at 240°C, flipping every 10 minutes, until turkey is golden brown and an instant-read thermometer inserted into thickest part of breast registers 165°C, 35 to 40 minutes. Let turkey rest about 10 minutes before slicing.

Nutritional Value (Amount per Serving):

Calories: 651; Fat: 19.74; Carb: 10.24; Protein: 103.58

Air Fryer Chicken Tenders

Prep Time: 15 minutes   Cook Time: 45 minutes   Serves: 4

Ingredients:

- 650g chicken tenders
- Kosher salt
- Freshly ground black pepper
- 2 and a half c. of panko breadcrumbs
- 1 and a half c. of all-purpose flour
- 2 large eggs
- 1/4 c. of buttermilk
- Olive oil cooking spray
- 1/3 c. of mayonnaise
- 2 tbsp of Dijon mustard
- 2 tbsp of honey
- 1/4 tsp of hot sauce (optional)

Directions:

1. Season chicken on both sides with salt and black pepper. Place panko and flour in separate shallow bowls. In a third bowl, whisk eggs and buttermilk. Working one at a time, dip chicken into flour, then egg mixture, and finally

into panko, pressing to adhere.

2. Working in batches, in an air-fryer basket, arrange chicken, being careful not to overcrowd. Spray tops of chicken with cooking spray. Cook at 240°C for 5 minutes. Flip chicken, spray tops with cooking spray, and continue to cook until golden brown, about 5 minutes more.

3. In a small bowl, whisk mayonnaise, mustard, honey, and hot sauce, if using; season with salt and black pepper.

4. Arrange chicken on a platter. Serve with honey mustard alongside.

Nutritional Value (Amount per Serving):

Calories: 736; Fat: 32.57; Carb: 73.67; Protein: 36.93

Air Fryer Turkey Meatloaf

Prep Time: 5 minutes   Cook Time: 35 minutes   Serves: 2-4

Ingredients:

- 2 tsp of extra-virgin olive oil
- 1 small yellow onion, finely chopped
- 3 cloves of garlic, minced
- 1/2 tsp of finely chopped rosemary
- 450g of ground turkey (preferably dark meat)
- 1/3 c. of fine breadcrumbs
- 1/4 c. of chopped fresh parsley leaves
- 1 large egg, beaten to blend
- 2 tsp of Worcestershire sauce
- 1 tsp of Dijon mustard
- 1/2 tsp of kosher salt
- 1/4 tsp of freshly ground black pepper
- Olive oil cooking spray
- 1/4 c. of ketchup
- 1 tbsp of light brown sugar

Directions:

1. In a medium nonstick skillet over medium-high heat, heat oil. Cook onion, stirring, until soft and golden, about 4 minutes. Add garlic and rosemary; cook, stirring, until fragrant, about 1 minute.

2. Scrape onion mixture into a medium bowl and let cool slightly. Add ground turkey, breadcrumbs, parsley, egg, Worcestershire, mustard, salt, and pepper and mix with your hands to combine. Divide turkey mixture in half. Form into 2 (5"-by-2 1/2") loaves.

3. Lightly coat an air-fryer basket with cooking spray. Place turkey loaves in basket. Cook at 240°C, flipping halfway through, until an instant-read

thermometer inserted into center registers 165°C, about 30 minutes.

4. In a small bowl, combine ketchup and brown sugar. Flip meatloaves and spoon glaze over top. Continue to cook at 240°C until glaze is set, about 5 minutes more.

Nutritional Value (Amount per Serving):

Calories: 346; Fat: 18.86; Carb: 11.93; Protein: 32.13

Air Fryer Chicken Thighs

Prep Time: 5 minutes   Cook Time: 25 minutes   Serves: 1

Ingredients:

- 4 chicken thighs
- 2 tsp of chicken seasoning

Directions:

5. Set the air fryer at 200°C.
6. Pat chicken thighs dry with some kitchen paper before adding a little oil and seasoning to coat them.
7. Put seasoned chicken thighs in the hot air fryer. Depending on the size of your air fryer you may need to do this in batches, or, if you can, use a trivet or shelf.
8. Cook for 10 minutes before turning the thighs over. Cook for a further 10 minutes. They should be crispy and cooked through - if they are not, return them to the air fryer for a further 5 minutes or until they are cooked. The internal temperature should be 75°C.
9. Serve with your favourite side dish!

Nutritional Value (Amount per Serving):

Calories: 1762; Fat: 129.28; Carb: 3.59; Protein: 137.4

Air Fryer Chicken Drumsticks

Prep Time: 5 minutes   Cook Time: 25 minutes   Serves: 1

Ingredients:

- 8 - 12 chicken drumsticks
- Oil (optional)
- Seasoning

Directions:

1. Set the air fryer at 200°C.
2. Optionally brush the drumsticks with some oil.
3. Season the chicken drumsticks with your favourite spices. You can just use salt if you prefer.

4. Add the drumsticks to the air fryer basket. You might need to use a trivet to fit them all in, or if you have a smaller air fryer, cook them in batches.
5. Cook for 22 - 25 minutes, turning halfway through.
6. Check the chicken is cooked all the way through - they should reach 75C internally, use a meat thermometer if possible.

Nutritional Value (Amount per Serving):

Calories: 2142; Fat: 124.1; Carb: 3.11; Protein: 235.17

Air Fryer Piri Piri Chicken Legs

Prep Time: 5 minutes   Cook Time: 22 minutes   Serves: 1

Ingredients:

- 4 chicken legs
- 2 tsp of Piri Piri spice mix
- 120g of Piri Piri marinade sauce (approx)

Directions:

1. Add the spice mix and sauce to the raw chicken legs. Leave them to marinate for around 30 minutes.
2. Transfer to the air fryer basket and cook at 190°C for 22 minutes.
3. Turn the chicken legs at the halfway mark.
4. The chicken legs are ready when the juices run clear and the internal temperature is 75°C – use a meat thermometer if necessary.

Nutritional Value (Amount per Serving):

Calories: 1382; Fat: 44.76; Carb: 19.47; Protein: 210.22

Air Fryer Chicken Nuggets

Prep Time: 10 minutes   Cook Time: 8 minutes   Serves: 1

Ingredients:

- 3-4 chicken breasts
- 2 eggs, beaten
- 100g of breadcrumbs, (approx)
- Seasoning of your choice, e.g., 1tsp of smoked paprika, 1tsp of garlic granules, 1/2 tsp of salt, 1/2 tsp of pepper.

Directions:

1. Cut chicken breasts up into small chicken nugget-sized chunks.
2. Set up a chicken nugget breading station of three bowls. Add the beaten egg to one bowl, mix the seasoning with the breadcrumbs, add to a

different bowl, and put the raw chicken pieces in another bowl.

3. Using kitchen tongs, dip the chicken in the beaten egg, then roll it in the seasoned breadcrumbs. Place in air fryer basket.
4. Repeat with each piece of chicken. Depending on the size of your air fryer, you may need to cook in 2 separate batches.
5. Cook at 200°C for 8 to 10 minutes. Check the chicken nuggets are cooked through before serving.

Nutritional Value (Amount per Serving):

Calories: 2889; Fat: 213.17; Carb: 2.12; Protein: 229.58

Air Fryer Chicken Parmesan

Prep Time: 10 minutes   Cook Time: 40 minutes   Serves: 4

Ingredients:

- 2 large boneless chicken breasts
- Salt
- Freshly ground black pepper
- 40g of plain flour
- 2 large eggs
- 100g panko breadcrumbs
- 25g of freshly grated Parmesan
- 1 tsp of dried oregano
- 1/2 tsp of garlic powder
- 1/2 tsp of chilli flakes
- 240g of marinara/tomato sauce
- 100g of grated mozzarella
- Freshly chopped parsley, for garnish

Directions:

1. Carefully butterfly chicken by cutting in half widthwise to create 4 thin pieces of chicken. Season on both sides with salt and pepper.
2. Prepare dredging station: Place flour in a shallow bowl and season with a large pinch of salt and pepper. Place eggs in a second bowl and beat. In a third bowl, combine bread crumbs, Parmesan, oregano, garlic powder, and chilli flakes.
3. Working with one piece of a chicken at a time, coat in flour, then dip in eggs, and finally press into panko mixture making sure both sides are coated well.
4. Working in batches as necessary, place chicken in basket of air fryer and cook at 200°C for 5 minutes on each side. Top chicken with sauce and mozzarella and cook at 200°C for 3 minutes more or until cheese is melty and golden.
5. Garnish with parsley to serve.

Nutritional Value (Amount per Serving):

Calories: 234; Fat: 6; Carb: 16.03; Protein: 28.65

Air Fryer Rotisserie Chicken

Prep Time: 20 minutes   Cook Time: 50 minutes   Serves: 6

Ingredients:

- 1chicken (1.3kg), cut into 8 pieces
- Salt
- Freshly ground black pepper
- 1 tbsp of dried thyme
- 2 tsp of dried oregano
- 2 tsp of garlic powder
- 2 tsp of onion powder
- 1 tsp of smoked paprika
- 1/4 tsp of cayenne

Directions:

1. Season chicken pieces all over with salt and pepper. In a medium bowl, whisk to combine herbs and spices, then rub spice mix all over chicken pieces.
2. Add dark meat pieces to air fryer basket and cook at 180°C for 10 minutes, then flip and cook 10 minutes more. Repeat with chicken breasts, but reducing time to 8 minutes per side. Use a meat thermometer to insure that chicken is cooked through, each piece should register 73°C.

Nutritional Value (Amount per Serving):

Calories: 199; Fat: 5.38; Carb: 1.97; Protein: 33.91

Air Fryer Orange Chicken

Prep Time: 10 minutes   Cook Time: 30 minutes   Serves: 4-6

Ingredients:

- 900g skinless chicken breasts, cut into 1" pieces
- 1/2 tsp of kosher salt
- 1/4 tsp of freshly ground black pepper
- 2 large eggs
- 1/4 c. of all-purpose flour
- 1/2 c. plus 1 tbsp of cornstarch
- Olive oil cooking spray
- 1 and a half c. of orange juice
- 1/4 c. of packed light brown sugar
- 2 tbsp of low-sodium soy sauce or tamari
- 2 tbsp of rice vinegar
- 2 cloves of garlic, minced
- 1/2 tsp of minced fresh ginger
- 1/4 tsp of crushed red pepper flakes
- 2 tsp of toasted sesame oil

- Sliced scallions and toasted sesame seeds, for serving

Directions:

1. In a medium bowl, pat chicken dry with paper towels; season with salt and black pepper. In a shallow bowl, beat eggs to blend. In another shallow bowl, whisk flour and 1/2 cup of cornstarch. Coat chicken in egg, then toss to coat in flour mixture, shaking off any excess.
2. Coat an air-fryer basket with cooking spray. Working in batches, arrange chicken in a single layer in basket; spray chicken with cooking spray. Cook at 240°C, tossing halfway through and spraying with cooking spray, until golden brown and cooked through, about 10 minutes. Transfer chicken to a clean large bowl.
3. In a measuring cup, whisk orange juice, brown sugar, soy sauce, vinegar, and remaining 1 tbsp of cornstarch.
4. Coat a small pot with cooking spray and heat over medium heat. Cook garlic, ginger, and red pepper flakes, stirring, until fragrant, about 2 minutes. Add orange juice mixture and bring to a boil. Cook, stirring occasionally, until thickened and slightly reduced, about 10 minutes (you should have about 1 1/4 cups sauce). Add oil and stir to combine.
5. Pour orange sauce over chicken and toss to coat. Garnish with scallions and sesame seeds.

Nutritional Value (Amount per Serving):

Calories: 400; Fat: 11.8; Carb: 25.69; Protein: 44.7

Air Fryer Chicken Wings

Prep Time: 5 minutes   Cook Time: 25 minutes   Serves: 1

Ingredients:

- 1 kg chicken wings
- 1 tbsp olive oil
- ½ tsp garlic powder
- ½ tsp onion powder
- ½ tsp paprika
- ½ tsp salt
- ½ tsp black pepper

Directions:

1. Set the air fryer temperature at 200°C.
2. Prepare the chicken wings by firstly patting them dry with some kitchen roll. The dryer the chicken wings are, the crispier they will come out.Add the wings to a large bowl and cover with the olive oil, tossing them so that they are all covered as much as possible.
3. Add all the seasonings, coating all the wings.
4. Put the chicken wings in the air fryer. Depending on how many wings you are cooking, and the size of your air fryer, you might need to do them in

batches. You can also use a rack in your air fryer to fit more in. The key thing is to make sure the wings are not touching each other so that they have room to crisp up.

5. Cook for 20 minutes, turning and shaking 2 or 3 times to ensure they cook evenly.
6. Increase the temperature to 200°C and cook for a further 5 minutes or until the skin is crispy.
7. Serve with BBQ sauce, Hot Pepper Sauce, Buffalo Sauce

Nutritional Value (Amount per Serving):

Calories: 2246; Fat: 140.43; Carb: 37.12; Protein: 197.42

Air Fryer Whole Roast Chicken

Prep Time: 5 minutes   Cook Time: 1 hour   Serves: 1

Ingredients:

- 1 whole chicken (up to 2kg, depending on the size of your air fryer)
- 1tbsp olive oil
- 1tsp smoked paprika
- 1tsp dried mixed herbs
- 1tsp garlic granules/salt

Directions:

1. Using a brush, coat the chicken in olive oil.
2. Mix the seasoning together and paste it all over the chicken. Make up some more spice mix if there isn't enough to coat the whole chicken.
3. Place the chicken in the air fryer basket, breast side down. Cook at 180°C for 45 minutes. Check on it once or twice to ensure it is cooking ok and not burning.
4. At 45 minutes, turn the chicken over so that it is breast side up. Cook for a further 15 minutes.
5. Check the chicken has cooked through. You can pierce it with a sharp knife to see if the juices run clear - or, my preferred way, use a meat thermometer to check the internal temperature. If it isn't cooked through, return it to the air fryer and cook for some more time, checking on it every so often.

Nutritional Value (Amount per Serving):

Calories: 913; Fat: 34.08; Carb: 2.18; Protein: 141.25

Air Fryer Chicken Breasts

Prep Time: 10 minutes   Cook Time: 20 minutes   Serves: 1

Ingredients:

- 2 chicken breasts (increase accordingly)
- 2 tbsp olive oil
- ½ tsp salt
- ½ tsp pepper
- ½ tsp garlic powder (or seasoning of your choice)

Directions:

1. Set the air fryer temperature at 180°C
2. Brush or spray each chicken breast with oil.
3. Season one side (the smooth side) of each chicken breast.
4. Place each chicken breast (smooth side down) in the air fryer basket. Season the other side.
5. Set the timer for 10 minutes.
6. After 10 minutes turn the chicken breasts over to allow them to cook on both sides.
7. Check the chicken is cooked all the way through - use a meat thermometer if necessary.
8. Leave the chicken to rest for 5 minutes before serving or slicing.

Nutritional Value (Amount per Serving):

Calories: 1251; Fat: 80.71; Carb: 3.29; Protein: 121.64

Chapter 4: Snacks and Appetizers

Air Fryer Tater Tots

Prep Time: 10 minutes   Cook Time: 1 hour 40 minutes   Serves: 55

Ingredients:

- 1.4kg of russet potatoes, peeled
- 1 and a half tsp of kosher salt
- 1/2 tsp of garlic powder
- 1/4 tsp of onion powder
- Freshly ground black pepper

Directions:

1. In a large pot of boiling water, add potatoes and boil until potatoes are met with only a little resistance when poked with a knife, about 7 minutes. Drain and let cool.
2. When potatoes are cool enough to handle, use medium holes on a box grater to shred potatoes. In a large bowl, combine shredded potatoes, salt, garlic powder, onion powder, and pepper. Use your hands to form about 2 tablespoons worth of mixture into a tater tot shape, gently squeezing mixture as necessary.
3. Working in batches, place tater tots in basket of air fryer. Cook on 240°C for 20 minutes, stopping to shake basket halfway through, until golden.
4. Remove from basket and sprinkle with salt.

Nutritional Value (Amount per Serving):

Calories: 22; Fat: 0.13; Carb: 4.63; Protein: 0.68

Air Fryer Kale and Feta Hand Pies

Prep Time: 15 minutes   Cook Time: 15 minutes   Serves: 18

Ingredients:

- 1 package (280g) frozen chopped kale or spinach, thawed and squeezed dry
- 1 spring onion, finely chopped
- 2 tbsp of chopped fresh dill
- 1 tsp of finely grated lemon zest
- 1/2 tsp of dried oregano
- 1/2 tsp of kosher salt
- 1/4 tsp of crushed red pepper flakes
- 1/4 tsp of freshly ground black pepper
- 1/4 tsp of garlic powder
- 1/4 c. of extra-virgin olive oil, divided
- 6 sheets of frozen phyllo dough (each sheet about 18"-by-13"), thawed according to package instructions
- 1 c. of crumbled feta (about 120g)

Directions:

1. In a medium bowl, combine kale, scallion, dill, lemon zest, oregano, salt, red pepper flakes, black pepper, garlic powder, and 1 tablespoon oil.
2. Cover phyllo with a slightly damp kitchen towel. Take 1 phyllo sheet and arrange on a clean work surface. Lightly brush phyllo all over with some of the remaining oil, then top with another sheet of phyllo. Lightly brush second sheet of phyllo all over with more oil. Slice layered phyllo crosswise into 6 long strips (about 13"-by-3" each).
3. Place 1 packed tablespoon kale mixture on corner nearest you on one strip of phyllo. Fold corner over kale mixture to make a triangle, then continue to fold (like folding a flag) until entire phyllo strip is completely folded over kale mixture. Transfer filled phyllo to a sheet tray and cover with a slightly damp kitchen towel. Repeat with remaining kale filling and phyllo. Brush outsides of phyllo with any remaining oil.
4. In an air-fryer basket, arrange 4 to 6 hand pies, spacing evenly apart and being careful not to overcrowd. Cook at 240°C, flipping halfway through, until golden and crisp, 10 to 12 minutes. Repeat with remaining hand pies. Serve warm or at room temperature.

Nutritional Value (Amount per Serving):

Calories: 61; Fat: 3.73; Carb: 4.93; Protein: 2.48

Air Fryer Caprese Stuffed Portobello Mushroom

Prep Time: 5 minutes   Cook Time: 20 minutes   Serves: 4

Ingredients:

- 1 large clove garlic, grated
- 2 tbsp of extra-virgin olive oil
- 1/2 tsp of kosher salt
- Freshly ground black pepper
- 4 portobello mushrooms (about 1 lb.), stems removed
- 120g of low-moisture mozzarella, cut into small pieces (about 3/4 c.), divided
- 8 cherry or grape tomatoes, halved (about 1/2 c.), divided
- Torn fresh basil leaves, balsamic glaze, and crushed red pepper flakes

Directions:

1. In a small bowl, whisk garlic, oil, 1/2 teaspoon of salt, and a few grinds of black pepper to combine. Brush mushrooms all over with oil mixture.
2. In an air-fryer basket, arrange 2 mushrooms domed side up. Cook at 240°C, turning domed side down halfway through, until tender, 7 to 9 minutes.

3. Carefully remove air-fryer basket. Fill caps with half of cheese and half of tomatoes; season with salt. Continue to cook at 240°C until cheese is melted and golden in spots and tomatoes are softened, 2 to 3 minutes more. Transfer to a plate. Repeat with remaining mushrooms, cheese, and tomatoes.
4. Arrange mushrooms on a platter. Top with basil, a drizzle of balsamic glaze, and red pepper flakes.

Nutritional Value (Amount per Serving):

Calories: 183; Fat: 11.09; Carb: 9.82; Protein: 13.17

Air Fryer Tuscan Stuffed Mushrooms

Prep Time: 10 minutes   Cook Time: 10 minutes   Serves: 2-4

Ingredients:

- 1/2 c. of thawed frozen chopped spinach, squeezed dry
- 1/4 c. of drained oil-packed sun-dried tomatoes (about 4 pieces), patted dry and finely chopped
- 60g of cream cheese, softened
- 2 tbsp of chopped fresh basil, plus more for garnish
- 1 tbsp of finely grated Parmesan
- 1/4 tsp of garlic powder
- 1/4 tsp of kosher salt
- Freshly ground black pepper
- 225g of cremini mushrooms
- 1 tbsp of Italian-style bread crumbs

Directions:

1. In a medium bowl, stir spinach, tomatoes, cream cheese, basil, Parmesan, garlic powder, salt, and a few grinds of pepper to combine.
2. Remove stems from mushrooms. On a work surface, arrange mushroom caps domed side down. Mound spinach mixture into each mushroom cap. Sprinkle top of spinach mixture with breadcrumbs.
3. In an air-fryer basket, arrange mushrooms stuffed side up. Cook at 240°C until mushrooms are tender and filling is hot, 8 to 10 minutes.
4. Arrange mushrooms on a platter. Garnish with basil.

Nutritional Value (Amount per Serving):

Calories: 339; Fat: 9.16; Carb: 63; Protein: 12.37

Air Fryer Broccoli Ranch Tots

Prep Time: 5 minutes   Cook Time: 25 minutes   Serves: 4

Ingredients:

- 1 () bag (280g) frozen broccoli, thawed
- 2 large eggs, beaten to blend
- 1 and a half c. of shredded cheddar
- 1 c. of panko bread crumbs
- 2 tbsp of ranch seasoning
- Olive oil cooking spray
- Ketchup

Directions:

1. Pat broccoli dry with paper towels. Transfer to a food processor and pulse until very finely chopped. Scrape broccoli into a medium bowl and stir in eggs, cheddar, panko, and ranch seasoning.
2. Using a tablespoon measuring spoon and lightly dampened hands, scoop out level tablespoonfuls of broccoli mixture and press into a tater tot shape. Transfer to a plate.
3. Lightly coat an air-fryer basket with cooking spray. Working in batches, arrange tots in a single layer in basket, spacing about 1/8" apart; spray with cooking spray. Cook at 240°C, turning halfway through and spraying with cooking spray, until crisp, 9 to 11 minutes.
4. Arrange tots on a platter. Serve warm with ketchup alongside.

Nutritional Value (Amount per Serving):

Calories: 127; Fat: 3.66; Carb: 18.03; Protein: 6.04

Air Fryer Sweet Plantains

Prep Time: 2 minutes   Cook Time: 16 minutes   Serves: 1-2

Ingredients:

- 2 very ripe (blackened) plantains, halved lengthwise, peeled
- 2 tsp of extra-virgin olive oil
- Kosher salt

Directions:

1. In a small bowl, toss plantains with oil. In an air-fryer basket, arrange plantains in a single layer. Cook at 240°C, tossing halfway through, until golden and very tender, 16 to 18 minutes; season with salt.

Nutritional Value (Amount per Serving):

Calories: 298; Fat: 4.29; Carb: 70.65; Protein: 1.83

Air Fryer Tostones with Creamy Mojo Dipping Sauce

Prep Time: 15 minutes   Cook Time: 35 minutes   Serves: 4

Ingredients:

- 2 medium green plantains
- Olive oil cooking spray
- 3 c. of warm water
- 2 and a quartee tsp of kosher salt, divided, plus more
- 1/2 tsp of plus 1 pinch of garlic powder
- 1/4 c. of finely chopped fresh cilantro
- 1/4 c. of plain full-fat Greek yogurt
- 1 tbsp of extra-virgin olive oil
- 1 tbsp of fresh lime juice
- 1 tbsp of fresh orange juice
- 1/4 tsp of ground cumin

Directions:

1. Trim and discard ends of plantains. Using a knife, slice a slit along length of plantain peel, avoiding flesh. Slice plantain crosswise into 1" rounds. Using your fingers or back of a spoon, remove peel from each slice; discard peel.
2. Lightly coat an air-fryer basket with cooking spray. Working in batches, arrange plantains in a single layer in basket. Cook at 240°C until just tender enough to smash and remain in one piece, about 6 minutes.
3. Transfer plantains to a work surface. Using bottom of a cup, flatten to a disk.
4. Meanwhile, in a large bowl, stir water, 2 teaspoons of salt, and 1/2 teaspoon of garlic powder until salt is dissolved. Soak tostones in water mixture 5 minutes, then pat dry with paper towels. Spray both sides of dried tostones with cooking spray.
5. Working in batches, in air-fryer basket, arrange tostones in a single layer. Cook at 400° until golden and crisp, about 7 minutes; season with salt.
6. In a small bowl, whisk cilantro, yogurt, oil, lime juice, orange juice, cumin, and remaining 1/4 tsp of salt and pinch of garlic powder until combined. Serve tostones with sauce alongside.

Nutritional Value (Amount per Serving):

Calories: 116; Fat: 5.19; Carb: 16.18; Protein: 1.4

Air Fryer Pizza Rolls

Prep Time: 10 minutes   Cook Time: 18 minutes   Serves: 1

Ingredients:

- 240g of natural/Greek yoghurt
- 350g of self-raising flour
- 200g of passata/pizza sauce (or enough to cover the dough)
- 150g of grated cheese
- 1tsp of dried herbs (optional)

Directions:

1. In a bowl, mix together the flour and yoghurt until a dough is formed. If the mixture is too wet and sticky, add in some more flour. If it is too dry, add in a little water. You need to be able to roll out the dough without it sticking or falling about.
2. On a lightly floured work surface roll out the dough into a rectangle.
3. Spread the pizza sauce/passata across the dough. You can use your favourite pizza sauce, or just some regular pasta sauce. Be careful it isn't too runny though or it will just run off the dough.
4. Sprinkle your grated cheese over the tomato sauce and add your favourite toppings.
5. Carefully roll the pizza over lengthwise until it is in a sausage shape.
6. Using a sharp knife, or a serrated knife, slice the pizza roll up into even slices.
7. Carefully place the pizza rolls in the air fryer basket. You might need to use a spatula to transfer them. I used a silicone baking liner but you can use baking paper or brush a little oil on your air fryer basket and add them direct.
8. Cook at 180°C for about 10 minutes. Check on them at 7 minutes and adjust the cooking time if needed. The pizza rolls are ready when the cheese has melted and the pizza dough has turned a golden colour.

Nutritional Value (Amount per Serving):

Calories: 1875; Fat: 37.73; Carb: 290.43; Protein: 87.81

Air Fryer Halloumi

Prep Time: 2 minutes   Cook Time: 8 minutes   Serves: 1

Ingredients:

- 225g of halloumi
- 1 tbsp of olive oil
- 1/2 tsp of dried thyme (optional)

Directions:

1. Set the air fryer at 200°C.
2. Slice halloumi and brush with oil on both sides. Sprinkle with seasoning if

using.

3. Transfer halloumi slices to the air fryer basket and air fry for 8 to 10 minutes, turning over halfway.
4. The halloumi is ready when it has softened and is beginning to turn brown around the edges.

Nutritional Value (Amount per Serving):

Calories: 120; Fat: 13.51; Carb: 0.1; Protein: 0.02

Air Fryer Chickpeas

Prep Time: 2 minutes   Cook Time: 15 minutes   Serves: 1

Ingredients:

- 1 can of chickpeas (400g), drained and rinsed
- 1 tbsp of olive oil
- 2 tsp of spice or herb seasoning

Directions:

1. Drain and rinse the chickpeas.
2. Add the oil and your choice of spices or herbs.
3. Toss the chickpeas until they are coated in the oil and seasoning.
4. Transfer to the air fryer basket and set off at 200°C, and air fry for 15 minutes, shaking two or three times.
5. The chickpeas should be hard and crispy when they are ready. If they are still a little soft, air fry them for a few more minutes. Add extra seasoning if required.

Nutritional Value (Amount per Serving):

Calories: 488; Fat: 19.77; Carb: 61.4; Protein: 18.14

Air-Fryer Sweetcorn Fritters

Prep Time: 15 minutes   Cook Time: 12 minutes   Serves: 10-12

Ingredients:

- 175g of plain flour
- 3/2 tsp of baking powder
- 1/2 tsp of garlic powder
- 1 tsp of smoked paprika
- 100ml of milk
- 2 eggs, beaten
- 1/2 small bunch of parsley, finely chopped
- 4 spring onions, finely chopped
- 500g of sweetcorn

Directions:

1. Combine the flour, baking powder, garlic powder, paprika and a good pinch

each of salt and freshly ground black pepper in a large bowl. Gradually whisk in the milk and eggs until you have a smooth, thick batter. Mix in the parsley, spring onions and sweetcorn. Make 10-12 fritters by taking a spoonful of the mixture (around the size of a golf ball) and flattening down. Put on a tray or plate.

2. Put a layer of baking parchment in the base of the air-fryer basket. Set the air-fryer to 200°C and cook the fritters in batches for 12-15 mins, turning after 8 mins until golden and set.

Nutritional Value (Amount per Serving):

Calories: 90; Fat: 2.15; Carb: 13.87; Protein: 3.81

Air Fryer Baked Potatoes

Prep Time: 2 minutes   Cook Time: 50 minutes   Serves: 4

Ingredients:

- 4 baking potatoes (about 250g each)
- 1/2 tbsp of sunflower oil
- toppings of your choice, such as butter, cheese, baked beans or tuna mayonnaise

Directions:

1. Scrub the potatoes, then pat dry with kitchen paper. Transfer to a plate, drizzle over the oil and rub it into the skins using your hands so the potatoes are well-coated. Season with salt and pepper – the salt will help the skins crisp up.

2. Arrange the potatoes in a single layer in an air fryer basket. Set the air fryer to 200°C and cook for 40-50 mins, or until a sharp knife goes through the potatoes easily. Check the potatoes after 20 mins – if they seem to be browning too quickly on one side, turn them over using tongs, then check again after another 20 mins to ensure they're cooked through. The size of the potato and model of air fryer may effect the cooking time. To speed up the cooking time, you can microwave on high for 8-10 mins before air frying (check after 15-20 mins). When ready, the skin should be crisp and the inside tender and fluffy. Split and serve immediately with the toppings of your choice.

Nutritional Value (Amount per Serving):

Calories: 295; Fat: 2.66; Carb: 58.57; Protein: 9.03

Air-Fryer Arancini

Prep Time: 15 minutes   Cook Time: 35-40 minutes   Serves: 4

Ingredients:

- 15g of unsalted butter
- 1 onion, finely chopped
- 1 large garlic clove, crushed
- 200g of risotto rice
- 700ml of hot chicken or vegetable stock
- 50g of Parmesan, finely grated,
- plus extra to serve
- 125g of mozzarella
- 100g of plain flour
- 2 eggs, beaten
- 100g of dried breadcrumbs
- olive oil spray, for misting

Directions:

1. Melt the butter in a large saucepan over a medium heat and cook the onion and garlic for 5 mins until softened. Stir in the rice and cook for 1 min, then add half the stock, stirring well.
2. Continue to cook the risotto for 20 mins, stirring frequently and adding more stock as it is absorbed, until the rice is tender and creamy. Stir in the parmesan, then season to taste. Spread out on a tray and leave to cool to room temperature.
3. Cut the mozzarella into 12 pieces and pat dry using kitchen paper.
4. Shape the risotto into 12 even-sized balls. Flatten one of the balls in the palm of your hand and add a piece of mozzarella. Bring up the edges to enclose it, then roll into a neat ball. Repeat to make 12 balls.
5. Roll each risotto ball in the flour, followed by the egg and finally the breadcrumbs until evenly coated. Chill until ready to air-fry, or until set and holding their shape well.
6. Set the air-fryer to 190°C. Mist the arancini with the olive oil spray and cook in batches for 10-15 mins until crunchy and golden brown. Scatter with parmesan before serving.

Nutritional Value (Amount per Serving):

Calories: 538; Fat: 23.26; Carb: 58.65; Protein: 24.85

Air-Fryer Spring Rolls

Prep Time: 5 minutes   Cook Time: 30 minutes   Serves: 8

Ingredients:

- 2 tbsp of cornflour
- 1 tbsp of dark soy sauce
- 1 tsp of honey
- 1 tsp of sesame oil

- 1 tbsp of vegetable oil
- 450g of mixed stir-fry vegetables (we used a mix of beansprouts, cabbage, carrots and peppers), any large pieces finely chopped
- 8 large or 16 small spring roll pastry sheets
- 2 tbsp of vegetable oil
- sweet chilli sauce, for dipping

Directions:

1. Mix 1 tbsp of the cornflour with the dark soy sauce until smooth, then add the honey and sesame oil. Set aside. Heat the vegetable oil in a wok over a high heat and stir-fry the mixed veg for 30 seconds before adding the sauce mixture. Season with salt and pepper, and cook for another minute until the veg has wilted slightly but retains some crunch. Transfer the mixture to a bowl and cool for at least 10 mins.
2. Mix the remaining cornflour with 1 tbsp of water in a small bowl. Working with one spring roll sheet at a time, put on a board at an angle, so it resembles a diamond. (Keep the other sheets covered with a tea towel.) Spoon a heaped teaspoonful of the veg in the centre of the sheet in a sausage shape. Fold the bottom corner over the filing and tuck it under. Fold in the left and right sides to neatly enclose the filling. Brush a little of the cornflour mixture over the top corner, then roll up from the bottom to seal. Put on a tray and brush with a little of the vegetable oil. Continue until you've assembled all the spring rolls.
3. Set the air-fryer to 200°C and cook the spring rolls for 12 mins, turning halfway through to brush with more oil. You may have to do this in batches – be careful not to overcrowd the air-fryer. Serve with the sweet chilli sauce for dipping.

Nutritional Value (Amount per Serving):

Calories: 187; Fat: 7.45; Carb: 24.76; Protein: 6.39

Air Fryer Pasta Chips

Prep Time: 5 minutes   Cook Time: 25-30 minutes   Serves: 4-6

Ingredients:

- 200g of pasta, such as farfalle
- 2 tbsp of extra virgin olive oil
- 2 tsp of smoked paprika
- 1 tsp of ground cumin
- large pinch of dried oregano
- 1 tsp of onion granules

Directions:

1. Cook the pasta following the packet instructions. Drain and transfer to a large bowl.
2. Add the olive oil, spices, herbs and season with salt and pepper, and mix

together so that the pasta is well coated.

3. Set your air fryer to 180°C and cook the pasta for 15-20 minutes, shaking every 5 minutes, until the pasta is crisp and golden. Serve the pasta chips on their own or with a dip.

Nutritional Value (Amount per Serving):

Calories: 173; Fat: 4.17; Carb: 36.39; Protein: 4.36

Air Fryer Toad in the Hole

Prep Time: 5 minutes   Cook Time: 17 minutes   Serves: 2

Ingredients:

- 1 to 2 tbsp of vegetable or sunflower oil
- 6 chipolatas
- 120g of plain flour
- 180ml of semi skimmed milk
- 2 eggs
- Pinches of salt and pepper

Directions:

1. Set your air fryer to 200°C.
2. Add the oil to a 20 cm baking tin and place it in the air fryer basket. Air fry for 3 minutes to heat the oil.
3. Carefully add the sausages to the baking tin and air fry for about 5 minutes until they begin to slightly brown.
4. While the sausages are browning, prepare the batter. Add the flour, milk, eggs and seasonings to a bowl and whisk until smooth and lump-free. Use an electric whisker if you have one.
5. When the sausages have browned enough, pour the batter over them. Try to do this step as quickly as possible to prevent too much heat from escaping.
6. Air fry for a further 12 minutes. The toad in the hole should be golden brown, and the batter should have risen above the sausages.

Nutritional Value (Amount per Serving):

Calories: 507; Fat: 19.68; Carb: 54.54; Protein: 26.67

Air Fryer New Potatoes

Prep Time: 5 minutes   Cook Time: 20 minutes   Serves: 4

Ingredients:

- 800g of new potatoes
- 1 to 2 tbsp of olive oil

- 1 tbsp of paprika (optional)   • Seasoning according to taste

Directions:

1. Chop the potatoes into even-sized chunks, halving the medium ones and quartering the large ones.
2. Place the potatoes in a large bowl, drizzle with olive oil and mix until all potatoes are well-coated. If you are seasoning with paprika (or other herbs/spices), add this now, ensuring it is evenly distributed.
3. Cook in the air fryer at 200°C for 20 minutes, shaking after 10 minutes.
4. The potatoes are ready when the skin is browned and crispy. If in doubt, use a sharp knife or skewer and pierce one potato to check it is soft all the way through.
5. Optionally garnish with chopped fresh coriander.

Nutritional Value (Amount per Serving):

Calories: 195; Fat: 1.9; Carb: 39.98; Protein: 4.61

Air Fryer Sweet Potato Fries

Prep Time: 5 minutes   Cook Time: 12 minutes   Serves: 2

Ingredients:

- 1 large sweet potato, approx 350g (makes 2 small portions, double up for more)
- 1 tbsp of olive oil (other oil of your choice, olive, coconut, avocado etc)
- 2 tsp of spice/seasoning mix (ideas include paprika, cayenne, garlic, pepper)
- Salt for seasoning once cooked (optional)

Directions:

1. Set the air fryer to 180°C.
2. Peel the sweet potato (optional).
3. Slice into thin chips.
4. Drizzle with oil, trying to cover as many fries as possible.
5. Sprinkle the spice mix over the fries and toss to coat.
6. Lay prepared fries in the air fryer basket.
7. Cook for 12 minutes, checking halfway to shake about/turn over. If the sweet potato fries aren't ready, return to the air fryer for a further 2 minutes before checking on them.

Nutritional Value (Amount per Serving):

Calories: 70; Fat: 6.8; Carb: 1.76; Protein: 0.14

Chapter 5: Fish and Seafood

Easy Baked Fish and Chips with Fried Brussels Sprouts

Prep Time: 15 minutes   Cook Time: 40 minutes   Serves: 4

Ingredients:

- 600g of maris piper potatoes, cut into 1cm slices
- Olive oil to coat/drizzle
- 4 sustainable white fish fillets such as sea bass or sea bream
- 40g of unsalted butter
- 450g of brussels sprouts, quartered (you can use leftovers if you have them)
- 1 tbsp of fennel seeds
- Finely grated zest and juice
- 1 lemon, plus wedges
- 2 tsp of caster sugar
- Chopped chives

Directions:

1. Set the air fryer to 200°C. Toss the sliced potatoes in olive oil and season well, then bake for 40 minutes or until golden and crisp.
2. When the potatoes have about 15-20 minutes left (depending on the size of your fish fillets), season and drizzle the fish with olive oil, and sit them on top of the potatoes in the oven.
3. Heat the butter in a large non-stick frying pan over a medium-high heat, then add the sprouts with some salt and cook for 3-4 minutes, tossing occasionally, until turning golden. Add the fennel seeds, lemon juice, zest and sugar, then continue to toss for another 3-4 minutes until caramelised and fragrant.
4. Once the fish is cooked and the potatoes are golden, divide among plates with a good spoonful of the cooked sprouts. Serve with lemon wedges and a scattering of chopped chives.

Nutritional Value (Amount per Serving):

Calories: 209; Fat: 6.14; Carb: 36.93; Protein: 5.39

Chilli Crab Jacket Potatoes

Prep Time: 10 minutes   Cook Time: 20 minutes   Serves: 2

Ingredients:

- Olive oil for coating and frying
- 2 medium baking potatoes
- 6 spring onions, finely sliced

- 20g of ginger, finely grated
- 2 garlic cloves, crushed
- 1 red chilli, deseeded and finely chopped
- 1 tbsp of dark soy sauce
- 1 and a half tbsp of tomato ketchup
- ½ tsp of rice vinegar
- 100g of pack white and brown crabmeat
- 60g of crème fraîche
- 10g of salted butter
- Green salad to serve

Directions:

1. Set the air fryer to 200°C. Rub a little oil over each potato and season with salt. Put directly on a shelf in the air fryer and bake for about 50 minutes. The potatoes are done when the skin is crisp and the potato is soft inside.
2. When the potatoes have 10 minutes' cooking left, put a little oil in a small pan over a medium heat. Once hot, add two thirds of the spring onions along with the ginger, garlic, two thirds of the chilli and a pinch of salt. Cook, stirring, for 1 2 minutes until soft. Add the soy sauce, ketchup and vinegar. Cook for 2 minutes, stirring, then remove from the heat.
3. Separate the white and brown crabmeat. In a bowl, mix the brown crabmeat with the crème fraîche, then stir in the chilli sauce mixture. Season to taste. Split open the baked potatoes and add the butter. Divide the chilli crab mixture between them, then top with the white crabmeat and the remaining spring onion and chilli. Serve with a green salad.

Nutritional Value (Amount per Serving):

Calories: 616; Fat: 23.39; Carb: 85.81; Protein: 10.09

Air Fryer Fish Tacos with Avocado Salsa

Prep Time: 5 minutes   Cook Time: 15 minutes   Serves: 4-6

Ingredients:

- 4 skinless cod filets (170g)
- 1 packet (28g) taco seasoning
- Olive oil cooking spray
- 1 ripe avocado, halved, pitted, and flesh scooped
- 1/2 c. of cool water
- 1/4 c. of chopped white onion
- 1/4 c. of packed fresh cilantro leaves
- 2 tbsp of fresh lime juice
- 1/2 tsp (or more) of kosher salt

- 1 jalapeño, stemmed, seeded and thinly sliced, divided
- 12 corn tortillas, warmed
- 1/2 c. of shredded red cabbage
- 1/2 c. of crumbled queso fresco or feta
- Lime wedges

Directions:

1. Pat cod dry with paper towels; season all over with taco seasoning.
2. Lightly coat an air-fryer basket with cooking spray. Working in batches, arrange cod in a single layer in basket, spacing about 1/2" apart; coat with cooking spray. Cook at 240°C, flipping halfway through, until cod is just cooked through and easily flakes with a fork, 6 to 8 minutes. Transfer to a plate.
3. Meanwhile, in a food processor, pulse avocado, water, onion, cilantro, lime juice, salt, and half of jalapeño until smooth; season with more salt, if desired.
4. Using a fork, flake cod into bite-sized pieces. Divide cod among tortillas. Top with avocado sauce, cabbage, queso fresco, and remaining jalapeño. Serve with lime wedges alongside.

Nutritional Value (Amount per Serving):

Calories: 296; Fat: 11.56; Carb: 36.9; Protein: 14.48

Air Fryer Miso Brown-Sugar Salmon

Prep Time: 10 minutes   Cook Time: 8 minutes   Serves: 1

Ingredients:

- 1 MOWI Atlantic Salmon Portion (170g)
- 1 tbsp of brown sugar
- 1 tsp of white miso
- 1/2 tsp of sesame oil
- 1/2 tsp of rice vinegar
- 1/2 tsp of soy sauce or tamari
- 1/4 tsp of ground ginger
- Salt and black pepper to taste
- 1/4 tsp of toasted sesame seeds
- Sliced scallions, for garnish

Directions:

1. Pat salmon dry and place in a shallow bowl; set aside.
2. In a small bowl, whisk together brown sugar, miso, sesame oil, rice vinegar, soy sauce, and ginger. Pour mixture over the salmon, turning to coat all sides. Cover and let marinate in the refrigerator for 30 minutes.

3. Set air fryer to 180°C and prepare basket by lining with foil. Remove salmon from marinade and transfer, skin-side down, to the foil-lined basket. Cook for 7 to 9 minutes, depending on the thickness of the fillet, or until the internal temperature reads 80°C for medium-well.
4. Season with salt and pepper, top with a sprinkling of toasted sesame seeds, and garnish with sliced scallions. Serve with rice or a side salad.

Nutritional Value (Amount per Serving):

Calories: 430; Fat: 15.31; Carb: 35.46; Protein: 37.42

Air Fryer Crab Cakes

Prep Time: 15 minutes   Cook Time: 15 minutes   Serves: 4

Ingredients:

- 1 large egg
- 1/4 c. of mayonnaise
- 2 tbsp of minced chives
- 2 tsp of Dijon mustard
- 2 tsp of Old Bay seasoning
- 1 tsp of finely grated lemon zest
- 1/2 tsp of kosher salt
- 450g of jumbo lump crab meat, picked over
- 1 c. of Saltine cracker crumbs (from about 20 crackers)
- Olive oil cooking spray
- 1/2 c. of dill pickle, finely chopped
- 1/4 c. of mayonnaise
- 1 tbsp of finely chopped shallot
- 2 tsp of capers, finely chopped
- 1 tsp of chopped fresh dill
- 1 tsp of fresh lemon juice
- 1/4 tsp of Dijon mustard
- Hot sauce and lemon wedges

Directions:

1. Crab Cakes: In a large bowl, whisk egg, mayonnaise, chives, mustard, Old Bay, lemon zest, and salt. Fold in crab meat and cracker crumbs until combined.
2. Form crab mixture into 8 patties (you can refrigerate patties up to 4 hours).
3. Spray an air-fryer basket and tops of crab cakes with cooking spray. Arrange crab cakes in a single layer in basket. Cook at 220°C, flipping halfway through, until deep golden brown and crisp, 12 to 14 minutes.

4. Tartar Sauce: In a medium bowl, stir pickles, mayonnaise, shallot, capers, dill, lemon juice, and mustard.
5. Serve crab cakes warm with hot sauce, lemon wedges, and tartar sauce.

Nutritional Value (Amount per Serving):

Calories: 481; Fat: 14.53; Carb: 47.69; Protein: 46.27

Air Fryer Blackened Tilapia with Mango Salsa

Prep Time: 10 minutes   Cook Time: 22 minutes   Serves: 4

Ingredients:

- 1 tbsp of finely ground cornmeal
- 2 tsp of dried oregano
- 2 tsp of sweet paprika
- 1 tsp of dark brown sugar
- 1 tsp of dried thyme
- 1 tsp of ground cumin
- 1/2 tsp of garlic powder
- 1 1/4 tsp of kosher salt, divided
- 1/2 tsp of freshly ground black pepper
- 4 tilapia filets (170g)
- Olive oil cooking spray
- 2 ripe mangoes, pitted, peeled, and chopped (about 2 1/4 c.)
- 1/2 large red bell pepper, finely chopped (about 1 c.)
- 1/2 small red onion, finely chopped
- 1/4 c. of chopped fresh cilantro leaves
- 1/4 c. of fresh lime juice
- 2 tbsp of extra-virgin olive oil

Directions:

1. In a small bowl, combine cornmeal, oregano, paprika, brown sugar, thyme, cumin, garlic powder, 3/4 teaspoon of salt, and 1/2 teaspoon of pepper. Pat tilapia dry with paper towels; generously season both sides with cornmeal mixture (use it all), pressing to adhere. Spray both sides of fish with cooking spray.
2. In an air-fryer basket, place 1 fillet. Cook at 240°C until just cooked through, 6 to 8 minutes. Repeat with remaining fish.
3. Meanwhile, in a medium bowl, combine mangoes, bell pepper, onion, cilantro, lime juice, oil, remaining 1/2 teaspoon of salt, and a few grinds of pepper.
4. Divide tilapia among plates. Top with mango salsa.

Nutritional Value (Amount per Serving):

Calories: 147; Fat: 5.13; Carb: 16.39; Protein: 10.91

Air Fryer Lemon-Garlic Shrimp

Prep Time: 5 minutes   Cook Time: 30 minutes   Serves: 4

Ingredients:

- 1 large garlic clove, grated or minced
- 1 tbsp of extra-virgin olive oil
- 1 tbsp of fresh lemon juice
- 1/2 tsp of Italian seasoning
- 1/4 tsp of crushed red pepper flakes
- 1/4 tsp of kosher salt
- 1/4 tsp of Worcestershire sauce
- 450g of large tail-on shrimp, peeled
- 1/2 lemon, thinly sliced into half moons, seeds removed
- 2 tbsp of finely chopped fresh parsley

Directions:

1. In a large bowl, whisk garlic, oil, lemon juice, Italian seasoning, red pepper flakes, salt, and Worcestershire sauce. Add shrimp and lemon slices and toss to coat.
2. Step 2
3. Working in batches, in an air-fryer basket, arrange shrimp and lemon slices in a single layer (do not overcrowd). Cook at 240°C until shrimp are opaque and cooked through, 10 to 12 minutes.
4. Step 3
5. Arrange shrimp and lemon slices on a platter. Top with parsley.

Nutritional Value (Amount per Serving):

Calories: 34; Fat: 1.73; Carb: 4.01; Protein: 0.89

Air Fryer Crab Cakes

Prep Time: 15 minutes   Cook Time: 15 minutes   Serves: 4

Ingredients:

- 60g of mayonnaise
- 1 egg
- 2 tbsp of chives, finely chopped
- 2 tsp of Dijon mustard
- 2 tsp of Cajun seasoning
- 1 tsp of lemon zest
- 1/2 tsp of salt
- 450g of jumbo lump crab meat
- 120g of Cracker crumbs
- Cooking spray
- Hot sauce
- Lemon wedges

- 60g of mayonnaise
- 80 g of dill pickle, finely chopped
- 1 tbsp of shallot, finely chopped
- 2 tsp of capers, finely chopped
- 1 tsp of fresh lemon juice
- 1 tsp of fresh dill, finely chopped

Directions:

1. Make crab cakes: In a large bowl, whisk together mayo, egg, chives, Dijon mustard, Cajun seasoning, lemon zest and salt. Fold in the crab meat and the cracker crumbs.
2. Divide the mixture equally, forming 8 patties. You can refrigerate them for up to 4 hours if you're not ready to fry them. (Patties can also be frozen on a parchment-lined baking tray.)
3. Set the air fryer at 190°C, and spray the basket and the tops of the crab cakes with cooking spray. Place the crab cakes into the basket in a single layer. Cook until deep golden brown and crisp, about 12-14 minutes, flipping halfway through.
4. Meanwhile, make tartar sauce: Combine all of the tartar sauce ingredients in a bowl.
5. Serve the crab cakes warm with hot sauce, lemon wedges, and tartar sauce.

Nutritional Value (Amount per Serving):

Calories: 656; Fat: 23.63; Carb: 67.34; Protein: 49.89

Air Fryer Coconut Shrimp

Prep Time: 5 minutes   Cook Time: 20 minutes   Serves: 4

Ingredients:

- 1/2 c. of all-purpose flour
- Kosher salt
- Freshly ground black pepper
- 1 c. of panko bread crumbs
- 1/2 c. of shredded sweetened coconut
- 2 large eggs, beaten
- 450g of large tail-on shrimp, peeled and deveined
- 1/2 c. of mayonnaise
- 1 tbsp of sriracha
- 1 tbsp of Thai sweet chili sauce

Directions:

1. In a shallow bowl, season flour with salt and black pepper. In another shallow bowl, combine panko and coconut. In a third shallow bowl, beat eggs to blend.
2. Working one at a time, dip shrimp into seasoned flour, shaking off any excess. Dip into eggs, then into panko mixture, gently pressing to adhere.

3. Working in batches if necessary, in an air-fryer basket, arrange shrimp in a single layer. Cook at 240°C until shrimp is golden brown and cooked through, 7 to 9 minutes.
4. In a small bowl, combine mayonnaise, sriracha, and chili sauce.
5. Arrange shrimp on a platter. Serve with dipping sauce alongside.

Nutritional Value (Amount per Serving):

Calories: 292; Fat: 16.88; Carb: 26.26; Protein: 8.45

Air Fryer Scallops

Prep Time: 20 minutes   Cook Time: 25 minutes   Serves: 4

Ingredients:

- 1 c. of seasoned panko breadcrumbs
- 1 tsp of Old Bay or Cajun seasoning
- 2 tbsp of butter, melted
- 450g of sea scallops
- Kosher salt
- 1 c. of all-purpose flour
- 1 egg, beaten
- 1 lemon, cut into wedges for serving
- 1 c. of mayonnaise
- 1 tbsp of Dijon mustard
- 1 tbsp of lemon juice
- 1 tbsp of Louisiana-style hot sauce (Louisiana, Frank's, Tabasco, Crystal, etc.)
- 1 tbsp of chopped parsley
- 1 spring onion, thinly sliced
- 1 clove of garlic, grated or minced
- 1 tsp of Old Bay or Cajun seasoning

Directions:

1. In a shallow bowl, combine bread crumbs and Old Bay until well combined. Drizzle in melted butter, gently tossing the panko with a fork to evenly incorporate the butter.
2. Pat the scallops dry and season all over with 1 teaspoon of salt. Place the flour, egg, and breadcrumbs in shallow bowls to create a dredge station. Coat a scallop in flour and tap off any excess. Then coat in the egg, then finally in the panko mixture. (Work with one dry hand and one wet hand to avoid extra mess.) Press the panko mixture into the scallop to ensure it adheres, and place it onto a paper towel-lined plate. Repeat with the remaining scallops. Place scallops in the refrigerator for 20 minutes,

uncovered.

3. Meanwhile, make the remoulade: In a small bowl, combine all of the remoulade ingredients and whisk until smooth. Cover with plastic wrap and refrigerate.

4. Brush the surface of the air fryer basket with neutral oil and set the air fryer to 240°C . Remove scallops from the refrigerator and check the breading for any wet spots. If there are wet spots, pat them gently with a bit of the panko mixture. Arrange half of the scallops in the air fryer basket so that none are touching, and cook for 3 minutes. Using tongs or a flexible spatula, gently flip each scallop and cook for an additional 3 minutes. The panko breading should be golden brown and feel crisp to the touch. Repeat with the remaining half. Serve immediately with remoulade and a lemon wedge.

Nutritional Value (Amount per Serving):

Calories: 641; Fat: 28.73; Carb: 55.59; Protein: 34.15

Air Fryer Salmon

Prep Time: 5 minutes   Cook Time: 10 minutes   Serves: 4

Ingredients:

- 1 tsp salt
- 1 tsp pepper
- 1 tsp mixed herbs
- 1 tsp garlic granules (optional)
- 4 salmon fillets (we used 4 x 130g fillets), skin on or removed
- ½ tbsp olive oil
- Cooked seasonal greens and grains such as quinoa or brown rice, to serve (optional)

Directions:

1. Combine the salt, pepper, mixed herbs and garlic granules, if using, in a bowl, then scatter onto a plate. Rub each salmon fillet with a little olive oil and roll in the seasoning to coat.

2. Put in the air fryer basket in one layer and cook at 180°C for 8-10 mins, until cooked through. If you have larger salmon fillets they will need to be cooked for longer – keep checking after 10 mins and cook in 1-2 min blasts, until ready. Serve with greens and quinoa or rice, if you like.

Nutritional Value (Amount per Serving):

Calories: 471; Fat: 18.9; Carb: 6.75; Protein: 69.56

Air Fryer Cod

Prep Time: 5 minutes   Cook Time: 10 minutes   Serves: 1

Ingredients:

- 2 cod fillets (approximately 150g each)
- 1 tablespoon olive oil
- ½ teaspoon paprika
- ½ teaspoon garlic powder
- Lemon wedges for serving
- Fresh parsley for garnish (optional)
- Salt and pepper to taste

Directions:

1. Pat dry the cod with a paper towel.
2. Mix the oil with the paprika and garlic powder in a small bowl and brush both sides of each fillet with the olive oil.
3. Place the seasoned cod fillets in the air fryer basket, ensuring they aren't overlapping.
4. Cook the cod in the air fryer at 200°C for about 10-12 minutes, or until the fish is opaque and flakes easily with a fork. The exact cooking time may vary depending on the thickness of your cod fillets, so it's a good idea to start checking for doneness around the 10 minute mark.
5. Carefully remove the cod fillets from the air fryer and serve with lemon wedges. Squeeze the lemon over the fish just before eating.
6. If you like, you can garnish the cod with fresh parsley before serving.

Nutritional Value (Amount per Serving):

Calories: 327; Fat: 15.05; Carb: 11.18; Protein: 37.77

Chapter 6: Vegan and Vegetables

Air Fryer Carrots And Chickpeas With Ricotta

Prep Time: 10 minutes   Cook Time: 22 minutes   Serves: 4-6

Ingredients:

- 400g of chantenay carrots or larger carrots, cut into 3cm chunks
- 400g of tin chickpeas
- 1 tbsp of olive oil
- 2 tsp of ras el hanout
- ½ tsp of chilli powder
- Finely grated zest and juice 1 lemon
- 500g of ricotta
- 2 tsp of runny honey, plus extra to drizzle
- Chopped parsley

Directions:

1. Set the air fryer to 180°C. In a bowl, toss together the carrots, chickpeas, olive oil, spices and a pinch of salt. Tip them into the air fryer basket and cook for 20 minutes, stirring halfway through.
2. Meanwhile, stir the lemon zest into the ricotta, season, then spread across a large serving platter. After the veg have been cooking for 20 minutes, drizzle the honey over the carrots and chickpeas, then cook for a further 2 minutes.
3. Scatter the chickpeas and carrots over the ricotta, then season with lemon juice, salt and a little more honey. Finish with the parsley.

Nutritional Value (Amount per Serving):

Calories: 546; Fat: 20.95; Carb: 63.94; Protein: 28.7

Air Fryer Primavera Roasted Vegetables

Prep Time: 5 minutes   Cook Time: 15 minutes   Serves: 2-4

Ingredients:

- 1 small summer squash, trimmed and sliced into 1/4"-thick rounds
- 1 small zucchini, trimmed and sliced into 1/4"-thick rounds
- 1 small red bell pepper, stemmed, seeded, and cut into 1" pieces
- 2 tsp of extra-virgin olive oil
- 1 tsp of finely chopped fresh rosemary
- 1/4 tsp of kosher salt
- 1/4 tsp of freshly ground black pepper
- 1/4 c. of grated Parmesan
- Chopped fresh parsley

Directions:

1. In a large bowl, toss squash, zucchini, bell pepper, oil, rosemary, salt, and black pepper. Scrape vegetable mixture into an air-fryer basket; reserve bowl. Cook at 240°C until vegetables are tender and golden in spots, about 12 minutes.
2. Return vegetables to reserved bowl and toss with Parmesan.
3. Divide vegetables among plates. Top with parsley and more Parmesan.

Nutritional Value (Amount per Serving):

Calories: 58; Fat: 2.34; Carb: 5.62; Protein: 4.33

Air Fryer Blooming Onion

Prep Time: 15 minutes   Cook Time: 30 minutes   Serves: 4

Ingredients:

- 1 large yellow onion
- 3 large eggs
- 1 c. of breadcrumbs
- 2 tsp of paprika
- 1 tsp of garlic powder
- 1 tsp of onion powder
- 1 tsp of kosher salt
- 3 tbsp of extra-virgin olive oil
- 2/3 c. of mayonnaise
- 2 tbsp of ketchup
- 1 tsp of horseradish
- 1/2 tsp of paprika
- 1/2 tsp of garlic powder
- 1/4 tsp of dried oregano
- Kosher salt

Directions:

1. Slice off onion stem and set onion on flat side. Cut an inch from the root down, into 12 to 16 sections, being careful not to cut all the way through. Flip over and gently pull out sections of onion to separate petals.
2. In a shallow bowl, whisk together eggs and 1 tablespoon water. In another shallow bowl, whisk together breadcrumbs and spices. Dip onion into egg wash, then dredge in breadcrumb mixture, using a spoon to fully coat. Drizzle onion with oil.
3. Place in basket of air fryer and cook at 240°C until onion is tender all the way through, 20 to 25 minutes. Drizzle with more oil as desired.
4. Meanwhile make sauce: In a medium bowl, whisk together mayonnaise, ketchup, horseradish, paprika, garlic powder, and dried oregano. Season with salt.
5. Serve onion with sauce, for dipping.

Nutritional Value (Amount per Serving):

Calories: 273; Fat: 20.99; Carb: 16.58; Protein: 5.52

Air Fryer Moroccan-Spiced Carrots

Prep Time: 10 minutes   Cook Time: 15 minutes   Serves: 2-4

Ingredients:

- 450g medium carrots, peeled, trimmed
- 1 tbsp of extra-virgin olive oil
- 1/2 tsp of ground cinnamon
- 1/2 tsp of ground coriander
- 1/2 tsp of ground cumin
- 1/2 tsp of kosher salt
- 1/2 tsp of smoked paprika
- 2 tbsp of fresh orange juice
- 2 tsp of fresh lemon juice
- 1/4 c. of pomegranate seeds
- 2 tbsp of chopped toasted almonds
- Torn fresh mint leaves

Directions:

1. In a medium bowl, toss carrots, oil, cinnamon, coriander, cumin, salt, and paprika. Scrape into an air-fryer basket; reserve bowl. Cook at 240°C until carrots are just tender, about 13 minutes.
2. In reserved bowl, combine orange juice and lemon juice. Add hot carrots and toss to coat. Top with pomegranate seeds, almonds, and mint.

Nutritional Value (Amount per Serving):

Calories: 113; Fat: 3.2; Carb: 21.13; Protein: 2.23

Air Fryer Asparagus

Prep Time: 5 minutes   Cook Time: 15 minutes   Serves: 2-4

Ingredients:

- 450g asparagus, tough ends removed
- 1 tsp of extra-virgin olive oil
- Kosher salt
- Freshly ground black pepper
- Lemon wedges

Directions:

1. In a medium bowl, toss asparagus with oil; season with salt and a few grinds of black pepper.
2. Working in batches if necessary, in an air-fryer basket, arrange asparagus in a single layer. Cook at 200°C until asparagus is tender, about 12 minutes.
3. Arrange asparagus on a platter. Serve with lemon wedges alongside.

Nutritional Value (Amount per Serving):

Calories: 67; Fat: 2.82; Carb: 6.92; Protein: 5.79

Air Fryer Zucchini

Prep Time: 10 minutes   Cook Time: 50 minutes   Serves: 4

Ingredients:

- 2 medium zucchini, sliced into 1/4" rounds
- 2 large eggs
- 3/4 c. of panko bread crumbs
- 1/3 c. of cornmeal
- 1/3 c. of freshly grated Parmesan
- 1 tsp of dried oregano
- 1/4 tsp of garlic powder
- Pinches of crushed red pepper flakes
- Kosher salt
- Freshly ground black pepper
- Marinara

Directions:

1. Place zucchini on a plate lined with paper towels and pat dry.
2. In a shallow bowl, beat eggs to blend. In another shallow bowl, combine panko, cornmeal, Parmesan, oregano, garlic powder, and red pepper flakes; season with salt and black pepper.
3. Working one at a time, dip zucchini rounds into egg, then into panko mixture, pressing to adhere.
4. Working in batches, in an air-fryer basket, arrange zucchini in an single layer. Cook at 200°C, flipping halfway through, until crispy on both sides, about 18 minutes. Serve warm with marinara.

Nutritional Value (Amount per Serving):

Calories: 145; Fat: 4.03; Carb: 20.17; Protein: 6.96

Air Fryer Falafel

Prep Time: 10 minutes   Cook Time: 35 minutes   Serves: 20

Ingredients:

- 1/2 yellow onion, cut into quarters
- 1/4 c. of packed cilantro leaves
- 1/4 c. of packed parsley leaves
- 4 cloves of garlic
- 450g tin chickpeas, rinsed and drained
- 2 tsp of ground cumin
- 1 tsp of baking powder
- 1 tsp of dried coriander
- 1 tsp of kosher salt, plus more
- 1/2 tsp of crushed red pepper flakes
- 1/3 c. of tahini

- Juice of 1/2 lemon
- 3 tbsp of water (or more)

Directions:

1. In a food processor, pulse onion, cilantro, parsley, and garlic, scraping down sides, until roughly chopped. Add chickpeas, cumin, baking powder, coriander, 1 teaspoon of salt, and 1/2 teaspoon of red pepper flakes. Pulse until chickpeas are mostly broken down with some chunks; stop just before mixture turns into a paste. Taste and adjust seasonings.
2. Scoop out about 2 tablespoons of chickpea mixture and gently form into a ball without squeezing too much or falafel will be dense. Working in batches, in an air-fryer basket, arrange balls. Cook at 240°C until browned, about 15 minutes.
3. Meanwhile, in a medium bowl, combine tahini and lemon juice. Add water and stir until combined, adding more water 1 tablespoon at a time until desired consistency is reached; season with salt and red pepper flakes.
4. Serve falafel as is with sauce, in a salad, or in a pita.

Nutritional Value (Amount per Serving):

Calories: 65; Fat: 3.36; Carb: 7.08; Protein: 2.44

Air Fryer Okra

Prep Time: 5 minutes   Cook Time: 25 minutes   Serves: 4

Ingredients:

- 2 tbsp of cornstarch
- 1 tbsp of Cajun seasoning (salt free, if possible)
- 1/4 tsp of kosher salt
- 450g of okra, halved lengthwise
- 2 tbsp of extra-virgin olive oil
- 1/2 c. of sour cream
- 2 tsp of creole mustard or country-style mustard
- 1/2 tsp of hot sauce
- Lemon wedges

Directions:

1. In a large bowl, combine cornstarch, Cajun seasoning, and 1/4 teaspoon of salt. Add okra and toss to coat. Drizzle with oil and toss again to coat.
2. Working in batches, in an air-fryer basket, arrange okra in a single layer (do not overcrowd). Cook at 240°C, tossing halfway through, until golden and crisp, about 18 minutes. Transfer okra to a plate; season with salt.
3. Meanwhile, in a small bowl, combine sour cream, mustard, and hot sauce; season to taste with salt, if desired.

4. Squeeze a lemon wedge over cooked okra. Serve with more lemon wedges and mustard sauce alongside.

Nutritional Value (Amount per Serving):

Calories: 156; Fat: 8.39; Carb: 14.88; Protein: 7.23

Air Fryer Green Beans

Prep Time: 10 minutes   Cook Time: 15 minutes   Serves: 4

Ingredients:

- 450g green beans, ends trimmed, cut into 3" segments
- 8 whole cloves garlic, peeled
- 2 tbsp of cornstarch
- 1 tbsp of extra-virgin olive oil
- 1 tbsp of reduced-sodium soy sauce or tamari
- 1/2 tsp of grated fresh ginger
- 1/4 tsp of ground white pepper
- 1/8 tsp of MSG (optional)
- Kosher salt
- Freshly ground black pepper

Directions:

1. In a large bowl, toss green beans, garlic, cornstarch, oil, soy sauce, ginger, white pepper, MSG (if using), 1/2 teaspoon of salt, and 1/2 teaspoon of black pepper until evenly coated.
2. In an air-fryer basket, arrange beans mixture in an even layer. Cook at 200°C until golden and tips are crispy, 10 to 12 minutes.

Nutritional Value (Amount per Serving):

Calories: 74; Fat: 2.58; Carb: 11.06; Protein: 2.84

Air Fryer Tempura-Inspired Green Beans

Prep Time: 10 minutes   Cook Time: 25 minutes   Serves: 4-6

Ingredients:

- 225g of green beans, trimmed
- 2 tbsp of all-purpose flour
- 1 c. of panko breadcrumbs
- 2 large eggs
- Olive oil cooking spray
- 1 spring onion, very thinly sliced
- 2 tbsp of water
- 1 tbsp of low-sodium soy sauce
- 1 tbsp of mirin
- 1 and a half tsp of fresh lemon juice

Directions:

1. In a large bowl, toss beans with flour until coated. In a shallow bowl, break up panko with your hands into smaller bits to help adhere to beans. In another shallow bowl, beat eggs to blend.
2. Shake off excess flour from beans. Dip into eggs, then into panko, gently pressing to adhere.
3. Working in batches, spray an air-fryer basket with cooking spray. Arrange beans in a single layer in basket, spacing about 1/4" apart; spray beans with cooking spray. Cook at 240°C, flipping halfway through, until crust is golden and beans are tender, 7 to 9 minutes.
4. In a medium bowl, whisk scallion, water, soy sauce, mirin, and lemon juice. Serve beans with sauce alongside.

Nutritional Value (Amount per Serving):

Calories: 68; Fat: 2.16; Carb: 10.43; Protein: 2.28

Air Fryer Aubergine

Prep Time: 5 minutes   Cook Time: 40 minutes   Serves: 4

Ingredients:

- 1 medium aubergine
- 1 tbsp of extra-virgin olive oil
- 1 tsp dried oregano
- 1/2 tsp garlic powder
- Pinches of crushed red pepper flakes
- Kosher salt
- Freshly ground black pepper
- Grated Parmesan, for serving

Directions:

1. Cut off ends of aubergine and cut in half lengthwise. Cut into strips 1" thick and 3" long. In a medium bowl, toss eggplant, oil, oregano, garlic powder, and red pepper flakes; season with salt and black pepper.
2. Working in batches, in an air-fryer basket, arrange aubergine in a single layer. Cook at 240°C , shaking basket halfway through, until golden, about 14 minutes. Top with Parmesan.

Nutritional Value (Amount per Serving):

Calories: 54; Fat: 2.41; Carb: 4.37; Protein: 3.81

Air Fryer Tofu

Prep Time: 10 minutes   Cook Time: 10 minutes   Serves: 1

Ingredients:

- 300g of firm tofu
- 2 tbsp of soy sauce

- 2 tsp of sesame oil
- 2 tsp of seasoning
- 2 tbsp of cornflour

Directions:

1. Cut the tofu into 1 inch size cubes using a sharp knife or kitchen scissors.
2. Place in a bowl and add the remaining ingredients, tossing everything together until the tofu is well coated.
3. Leave the tofu to marinate for 5 to 10 minutes. During this time, you can set the air fryer at 200°C.
4. Transfer the marinated tofu to the air fryer basket and cook for 10 minutes. Shake the basket at 5 minutes to ensure the tofu crisps all the way over.
5. Serve alone or with your favourite dip.

Nutritional Value (Amount per Serving):

Calories: 625; Fat: 40.93; Carb: 24.04; Protein: 49.87

Air Fryer Broccoli

Prep Time: 10 minutes   Cook Time: 10 minutes   Serves: 4

Ingredients:

- 1 medium head broccoli, cut into florets
- 1 tbsp of extra-virgin olive oil
- 1 clove of garlic, crushed
- Salt
- Freshly ground black pepper
- Pinches of chilli flakes

Directions:

1. In a large bowl, toss broccoli with oil and garlic. Season with salt, pepper, and chilli flakes.
2. Working in batches if necessary, add broccoli to basket of air fryer in a single layer. Cook at 180°C until tender and crisp, about 10 minutes. Repeat with remaining broccoli.

Nutritional Value (Amount per Serving):

Calories: 67; Fat: 4.29; Carb: 5.55; Protein: 2.72

Air Fryer Cauliflower

Prep Time: 5 minutes   Cook Time: 15 minutes   Serves: 2

Ingredients:

- 2 tbsp of ghee or butter, melted

- 1/2 tsp of garlic powder
- 1/4 tsp of turmeric
- 1 small head of cauliflower cut into small florets
- Salt
- Freshly ground black pepper

Directions:

1. In a small bowl whisk together ghee, garlic powder, and turmeric. Place cauliflower in a large bowl and pour over the ghee mixture, tossing to coat until all the florets are tinted yellow. Season generously with salt and pepper.
2. Set the air fryer temperature at 190°C. Add cauliflower to air fryer basket in a single layer and cook, tossing halfway through, until golden brown, 10 to 12 minutes.

Nutritional Value (Amount per Serving):

Calories: 154; Fat: 12.95; Carb: 7.44; Protein: 4.12

Air Fryer Courgette

Prep Time: 10 minutes   Cook Time: 50 minutes   Serves: 4

Ingredients:

- 2 medium courgette, sliced into 1/2cm rounds
- 2 large eggs
- 90g of panko bread crumbs
- 50g of polenta
- 35g of freshly grated Parmesan
- 1 tsp of dried oregano
- 1/4 tsp of garlic powder
- Pinches of chilli flakes
- Salt
- Freshly ground black pepper
- Marinara

Directions:

1. Place cut courgette on a platter lined with paper towels and pat dry.
2. Place beaten eggs in a shallow bowl. In another shallow bowl, combine panko, cornmeal, Parmesan, oregano, garlic powder, and a large pinch of chilli flakes. Season with salt and pepper.
3. Working one at a time, dip courgette rounds into egg, then into panko mixture, pressing to coat.
4. Working in batches as needed, place courgette in an even layer and cook at 200°C for 18 minutes, flipping halfway through. Serve warm with

marinara.

Nutritional Value (Amount per Serving):

Calories: 372; Fat: 15.95; Carb: 21.98; Protein: 33.3

Air Fryer Brussels Sprouts

Prep Time: 10 minutes   Cook Time: 20 minutes   Serves: 4

Ingredients:

- 450g of Brussels sprouts, trimmed and cut in half
- 1 tbsp of extra-virgin olive oil
- Salt
- Freshly ground black pepper
- Pinch crushed chilli flakes
- Juice of 1/2 lemon
- 1 tbsp of honey
- 1 tbsp of red wine vinegar
- 2 tsp of Dijon mustard
- 1 clove of garlic, crushed

Directions:

1. In a medium bowl, add brussels sprouts and oil and season with salt, pepper, and chilli flakes. Toss around to coat brussels sprouts well.
2. Add brussels sprouts to basket of air fryer, working in batches as needed, and cook at 190°C for 18 minutes, stopping and tossing brussels in basket halfway through.
3. Meanwhile, make dressing: In a small bowl, whisk together lemon juice, honey, vinegar, mustard, and garlic. Season with salt and pepper.
4. Add cooked Brussels sprouts back to a medium bowl and pour dressing over and toss to combine.

Nutritional Value (Amount per Serving):

Calories: 122; Fat: 4.45; Carb: 18.89; Protein: 4.86

Air Fryer Fried Pickles

Prep Time: 10 minutes   Cook Time: 45 minutes   Serves: 3

Ingredients:

- 300g of dill pickle slices
- 1 egg, whisked with 1 tbsp water
- 50g of breadcrumbs
- 25g of freshly grated Parmesan
- 1 tsp of dried oregano
- 1 tsp of garlic powder

- Ranch, for dipping

Directions:

1. Using paper towels, pat pickle chips dry. In a medium bowl, stir together breadcrumbs, Parmesan, oregano, and garlic powder.
2. Dredge pickle chips first in egg and then in the bread crumb mixture. Working in batches, place in a single layer in air fryer basket. Cook at 200°C for 10 minutes.
3. Serve warm with ranch.

Nutritional Value (Amount per Serving):

Calories: 104; Fat: 4.85; Carb: 8.12; Protein: 7.32

Air-Fryer Cauliflower Popcorn with Soured Cream & Herb Dressing

Prep Time: 20 minutes   Cook Time: 20 minutes   Serves: 4

Ingredients:

- 1 medium cauliflower (about 1kg)
- 125g of plain flour
- 25g of Parmesan or vegetarian alternative, grated
- 1 tsp of onion granules
- 1/2 tsp of dried oregano
- 1 tsp of paprika
- 1 egg
- 150ml of milk
- 80g of panko breadcrumbs
- olive oil, for drizzling (optional)
- 150ml of soured cream
- Pinches of onion granules
- 10g of chives, chopped

Directions:

1. Make the dip first by combining the soured cream, onion granules, some seasoning and all but 1 tbsp of the chives. Mix to combine, spoon into a small serving bowl and scatter over the reserved chives. Chill until needed. Will keep chilled for 24 hrs.
2. Cut the cauliflower into small florets and set aside. Combine the flour, parmesan, onion granules, dried oregano and paprika in a bowl, then mix in the egg and as much milk as you need to create a thick batter. Season well and set aside. Tip the breadcrumbs onto a plate. Dip the florets into the batter, shake off any excess, then roll in the breadcrumbs to coat.

Transfer to a plate.

3. Set the air-fryer to 200°C , then put the cauliflower in the basket in a single layer (you'll need to cook in batches) and cook for 15-20 mins until golden and crisp. Alternatively, to cook in the oven, drizzle over a little olive oil and bake at 200°C/180°C fan/gas 6 for 20 mins until golden and crisp. Serve straightaway with the dip.

Nutritional Value (Amount per Serving):

Calories: 406; Fat: 17.61; Carb: 49.39; Protein: 15.09

Air-Fryer Clementine & Chilli Halloumi Skewers

Prep Time: 20 minutes   Cook Time: 6-8 minutes   Serves: 10

Ingredients:

- 1 clementine, zested and juiced
- 3 tbsp of marmalade (clementine, if possible)
- 1 tbsp of triple sec (optional)
- Chilli flakes
- 2 tsp of vegetable oil
- 500g halloumi
- Sweet chilli sauce or sriracha mayo

Directions:

1. Put all of the ingredients except the halloumi and chilli sauce in a bowl with a good pinch each of salt and freshly ground black pepper. Mix together, then set aside.

2. Cut both of the halloumi blocks down the centre through the natural split, then cut each half into eight cubes (you'll have about 32 in total). Put the halloumi in the bowl with the clementine marinade, stir to coat, then cover and chill for at least 3 hrs, or overnight.

3. Remove the halloumi from the marinade, then thread about three blocks onto a mini metal skewer. The uncooked skewers will keep frozen in an airtight container for up to three months. Set the air-fryer to 200°C. Cook the skewers in a single layer for 6-8 mins until golden, turning halfway. If frozen, cook for 5 mins at 180°C, then a further 4-6 mins at 200°C. Serve with your choice of dip.

Nutritional Value (Amount per Serving):

Calories: 143; Fat: 8.5; Carb: 9.67; Protein: 7.17

Air-Fryer Mushrooms on Toast

Prep Time: 5 minutes   Cook Time: 12-15 minutes   Serves: 2

Ingredients:

- 300g of chestnut mushrooms, quartered or sliced
- a few thyme sprigs, leaves picked
- 1/2 tsp of garlic powder
- 1 tbsp of vegetable oil or other neutral oil, plus extra for the bread
- 2 slices of sourdough
- 1 garlic clove, peeled but left whole (optional)
- small handful of chopped parsley (optional)

Directions:

1. Tip the mushrooms into a bowl, scatter over the thyme leaves and garlic powder, and season. Stir everything together to combine. Drizzle over the oil and mix again.
2. Set the air-fryer to 200°C. Tip the mushrooms into the basket and cook for 12-15 mins, mixing up halfway through, until golden and beginning to crisp up.
3. A few minutes before the end of cooking, toast the bread. If you like, you can rub the toast with a garlic clove for extra flavour. Drizzle with a little oil, then spoon over the mushrooms. Scatter with parsley, if you like.

Nutritional Value (Amount per Serving):

Calories: 769; Fat: 18.32; Carb: 122.75; Protein: 51.47

Chapter 7: Desserts

Air Fryer Halloumi with Spiced Honey Glaze

Prep Time: 10 minutes   Cook Time: 15 minutes   Serves: 2

Ingredients:

- 225g of block halloumi, cut into thick slices
- 1 tsp of olive oil
- 2 tbsp of runny honey
- 1 tsp of nigella seeds
- Pinch of chilli flakes
- Finely grated zest 1/2 lemon

Directions:

1. Pat the halloumi dry, then coat with the oil. Set your air fryer to 180°C, then put the halloumi in it. Cook for 8 minutes, turning halfway.
2. Meanwhile, if you're making the dressing, combine all the ingredients and when the halloumi is cooked, drizzle half the dressing over the pieces and return to the air fryer for 1 minute, then serve drizzled with the remaining dressing.

Nutritional Value (Amount per Serving):

Calories: 360; Fat: 19.33; Carb: 26.54; Protein: 22.48

Air Fryer Doughnuts with Quick Berry Compote

Prep Time: 10 minutes   Cook Time: 35 minutes   Serves: 8

Ingredients:

- 2 medium free-range eggs
- 250g of ricotta
- 1 tsp of vanilla extract
- 50g of caster sugar, plus 1 tbsp
- 200g of self-raising flour
- 250g of frozen mixed berries
- Icing sugar to dust

Directions:

1. Crack the eggs into a mixing bowl, lightly beat, then stir in the ricotta, vanilla and caster sugar. Fold in the flour to create a thick batter.
2. Set the air fryer to 200°C. Use 2 dessert spoons to scoop the batter into 8 balls, adding them to the air fryer basket in a single layer with plenty of space between each (cook in batches if needed). Cook for 6-7 minutes until golden and crisp.
3. Meanwhile, put the berries in a pan with 1 tbsp of caster sugar. Bring to a simmer, then bubble for about 6 minutes until broken down into a compote. Serve the doughnuts warm and dusted with icing sugar, with the berry compote for dunking.

Nutritional Value (Amount per Serving):

Calories: 315; Fat: 8.99; Carb: 45.81; Protein: 11.78

Air Fryer Quiche

Prep Time: 20 minutes   Cook Time: 55 minutes   Serves: 4

Ingredients:

- 3 medium free-range eggs
- 170ml of evaporated milk
- 160g of cheddar, coarsely grated
- 3 thyme sprigs
- 1/2 small broccoli
- 175g of plain flour, plus extra to dust
- 115g of unsalted butter, chilled and chopped, plus extra to grease
- 20ml of whole milk
- 1 tsp of white wine vinegar
- 1 small free-range egg, beaten

Directions:

1. To make the pastry, put the flour and a pinch of salt in a mixing bowl. Rub in the butter using your fingers and thumbs until the mixture resembles coarse breadcrumbs. Stir in the milk, vinegar and most of the egg, cutting it into the flour mixture with a knife, then use your hands to briefly work the mixture until it comes together in a dough. Shape into a ball, flatten into a disc, cover and chill in the fridge for 30 minutes.
2. Meanwhile, set the air fryer to 180°C. Chop the broccoli into florets then fry for 8 minutes until coloured and slightly tender. Set aside.
3. Grease the tin with a little butter, then roll the pastry out on a floured work surface into a circle slightly larger than your tin. Use it to line the tin, ensuring the pastry comes up the sides, then use a fork to prick the base. Cover the pastry with baking paper, fill with baking beans or raw rice, then blind bake in the air fryer for 10 minutes at 180°C.

Nutritional Value (Amount per Serving):

Calories: 457; Fat: 36.06; Carb: 9.63; Protein: 24.65

Air Fryer Vegan Chocolate Zucchini Birthday Cake

Prep Time: 10 minutes   Cook Time: 1 hour 10 minutes   Serves: 4

Ingredients:

- 2 tbsp of neutral oil, such as avocado or vegetable, plus more for pan

- 3/4 c. all-purpose flour
- 1/2 c. vegan granulated sugar
- 3 tbsp of dark unsweetened cocoa powder
- 1 tsp of instant espresso powder
- 1/2 tsp of baking soda
- 1/4 tsp of kosher salt
- 1/2 c. of almond milk creamer or regular almond milk
- 1 tsp of pure vanilla extract
- 3/4 c. of shredded zucchini (from 1 small zucchini)
- 1 tbsp of apple cider vinegar
- 3/4 c. of vegan powdered sugar
- 2 tbsp of margarine, room temperature
- 1 tbsp of almond milk creamer or almond milk
- 1 tsp of dark unsweetened cocoa powder
- 1/2 tsp pure vanilla extract
- Sprinkles, for serving (optional)

Directions:

1. Brush a 7" nonstick round pan with oil. Line pan with parchment paper; brush parchment with oil. In a medium bowl, whisk flour, granulated sugar, cocoa powder, espresso powder, baking soda, and salt to combine. Add creamer, vanilla, and oil and stir to combine. Add zucchini and vinegar and gently fold to combine.
2. Immediately scrape batter into prepared pan, smoothing top. Place pan in an air-fryer basket. Cook at 240°C until cake is puffed and a tester inserted into center comes out clean, 30 to 35 minutes.
3. Let cake cool in pan 5 minutes, then invert onto a wire rack and remove parchment. Let cool completely.
4. Using an electric mixer on medium-high speed, in a large bowl, beat powdered sugar, margarine, creamer, cocoa powder, and vanilla until smooth and fluffy, about 2 minutes.
5. Spread frosting over cake. Decorate with sprinkles, if using.

Nutritional Value (Amount per Serving):

Calories: 363; Fat: 14.35; Carb: 54.71; Protein: 6.2

Air Fryer Apple Pie Baked Apples

Prep Time: 5 minutes   Cook Time: 25 minutes   Serves: 2

Ingredients:

- 3 Pink Lady apples
- 2 tbsp of granulated sugar

- 1 tsp of cornflour
- 1/2 tsp ground cinnamon
- 1/4 c. of water
- 1 tsp of fresh lemon juice
- All-purpose flour, for dusting
- 1 refrigerated pie crust
- 1 large egg, beaten to blend
- Caramel sauce, for drizzling (optional)

Directions:

1. Peel and finely chop 1 apple. Transfer to a small pot. Add sugar, cornstarch, and cinnamon and toss to coat. Add water and lemon juice, then bring to a simmer over medium heat. Cook, stirring frequently, until apples are tender and liquid thickens, about 10 minutes.
2. Meanwhile, slice off top 1/2" of remaining 2 apples. Hollow out apples with a melon baller or teaspoon. Arrange apples on a work surface and fill with cooked apple mixture.
3. On a lightly floured surface, roll out dough to 1/8" thick. Cut out 2 (4") circles. Slice each circle into scant 1/4"-thick strips. Arrange strips in a lattice pattern over each apple, pressing outer edges into apple and trimming any excess.
4. Brush dough with egg; sprinkle with sugar and cinnamon. Place apples in an air-fryer basket. Cook at 240°C until tender, filling is bubbling, and crust is golden, about 14 minutes. Let cool slightly before drizzling with caramel sauce, if using.

Nutritional Value (Amount per Serving):

Calories: 711; Fat: 27.36; Carb: 109.6; Protein: 10.6

Air Fryer Cinnamon Rolls

Prep Time: 5 minutes   Cook Time: 25 minutes   Serves: 6

Ingredients:

- 2 tbsp of melted butter, plus more for brushing
- 1/3 c. of packed brown sugar
- 1/2 tsp of ground cinnamon
- Kosher salt
- All-purpose flour, for surface
- 1 tube (220g) refrigerated Crescent rolls
- 2 oz. of cream cheese, softened
- 1/2 c. of powdered sugar
- 1 tbsp of whole milk, plus more if needed

Directions:

1. Make rolls: Line bottom of air fryer with parchment paper and brush with butter. In a medium bowl, combine butter, brown sugar, cinnamon, and a large pinch of salt until smooth and fluffy.
2. On a lightly floured surface, roll out crescent rolls in one piece. Pinch seams together and fold in half. Roll into a 9"-x-7" rectangle. Spread butter mixture over dough, leaving 1/4-inch border. Starting at a long edge, roll up dough like a jelly roll, then cut crosswise into 6 pieces.
3. Arrange pieces in prepared air fryer, cut-side up, spaced evenly.
4. Set air fryer to 240°C, and cook until golden and cooked through, about 10 minutes.
5. Make the glaze: In a medium bowl, Whisk cream cheese, powdered sugar, and milk together. Add more milk by the teaspoonful, if necessary, to thin glaze.
6. Spread glaze over warm cinnamon rolls and serve.

Nutritional Value (Amount per Serving):

Calories: 174; Fat: 7.04; Carb: 25.63; Protein: 2.52

Air Fryer Grilled Cheese

Prep Time: 2 minutes   Cook Time: 10 minutes   Serves: 1

Ingredients:

- 2 slices of bread such as white, sourdough or wheat
- 2 tsp of mayonnaise or softened salted butter, divided
- 4 slices of melty cheese such as American, Cheddar or Colby Jack

Directions:

1. Process all of the ingredients through your juicer and then dispense into your
2. Spread 1 teaspoon of mayo on one side of each piece of bread, edge to edge. Build a sandwich by placing cheese in between the two pieces of bread, mayo side out.
3. Place a piece of parchment that is slightly larger than the sandwich in the air fryer basket. Place the sandwich on the parchment.
4. Set the air fryer to 240°C, and cook for 8 minutes, flipping once, or until the cheese is melted and the bread is golden and toasted. Slice and serve.

Nutritional Value (Amount per Serving):

Calories: 305; Fat: 17.01; Carb: 25.15; Protein: 14.69

Air Fryer Pumpkin Biscuits

Prep Time: 10 minutes   Cook Time: 10 minutes   Serves: 4

Ingredients:

- 1 c. of all-purpose flour, plus more for surface
- 1 tbsp of light brown sugar
- 1 tsp of baking powder
- 3/4 tsp of pumpkin spice
- 1/2 tsp of kosher salt
- 4 tbsp of cold unsalted butter, cut into cubes, plus 1 tbsp of melted for brushing
- 1/4 c. of canned pure pumpkin puree
- 2 tbsp of buttermilk

Directions:

1. In a medium bowl, whisk flour, sugar, baking powder, pumpkin spice, and salt. Using a fork or 2 table knives, work cubed butter into flour mixture until it resembles a coarse meal.
2. In a liquid measuring cup or another medium bowl, whisk pumpkin puree and buttermilk until combined. Pour into flour mixture and stir with a fork until just combined and a shaggy dough forms.
3. Turn the dough out onto a lightly floured work surface. Gently knead dough with your hands until no dry spots remain. Pat dough into a 4"-by-4" square and cut into 4 squares. Brush tops of squares with melted butter.
4. In an air-fryer basket, arrange dough squares in a single layer. Cook at 240°C, tenting with foil during the last 3 minutes to prevent overbrowning if necessary, until golden and risen, 10 to 12 minutes.

Nutritional Value (Amount per Serving):

Calories: 207; Fat: 8.7; Carb: 27.95; Protein: 4.5

Air Fryer Coconut Macaroons

Prep Time: 5 minutes   Cook Time: 40 minutes   Serves: 4-6

Ingredients:

- 2 large egg whites
- 4 tsp of honey
- Pinches of kosher salt
- 1 and a half c. of unsweetened shredded coconut
- Olive oil cooking spray
- 1/2 c. of semisweet chocolate chips

- 1 tsp of virgin coconut oil

Directions:

1. In a medium bowl, whisk egg whites, honey, and salt until foamy. Add coconut and stir to combine.
2. Line an air-fryer basket with foil, leaving about a 1" overhang on 2 opposite sides. Lightly coat foil with cooking spray.
3. Tightly pack coconut mixture into a tablespoon measuring spoon. Carefully arrange mounds flat side down in prepared basket, spacing about 1/4" apart. Cook at 240°C until set on top and light golden in places, 5 to 7 minutes. Flip and continue to cook until flat side are set and dry to the touch, 1 to 2 minutes more. Using foil overhang, carefully remove macaroons from air fryer. Let cool.
4. Line a small baking sheet or plate with parchment. In a small heatproof bowl, combine chips and oil. Microwave on high, stirring, until just melted and smooth, about 1 minute.
5. Dip flat side of macaroons into chocolate mixture. Transfer to prepared sheet chocolate side down. Refrigerate until chocolate is set, about 20 minutes.

Nutritional Value (Amount per Serving):

Calories: 193; Fat: 10.92; Carb: 24.63; Protein: 2.71

Air Fryer Apple Crumble

Prep Time: 10 minutes   Cook Time: 25 minutes   Serves: 1

Ingredients:

- 2 large Bramley apples
- 250g of plain flour
- 1 tsp of ground cinnamon
- 150g of butter
- 75g of brown sugar

Directions:

1. Peel and chop the apples into small chunks and place them in an air fryer safe baking tin. Sprinkle 2 tablespoons of water over the top of them.
2. Air fryer at 180°C for 15 minutes, or until the apple chunks soften.
3. While the apples are in the air fryer, you can make the crumble mixture. In a mixing bowl, combine the flour and butter. Using your hands, rub it together until it resembles breadcrumbs and then add the sugar and ground cinnamon, stirring it in. Alternatively, you can use a food processor but be careful not to over-process; the crumble needs to have enough texture and not be too fine.
4. When the apples are ready, add the crumble mixture on top.
5. Close the air fryer basket and continue to air fry at the same temperature

for a further 10 minutes, checking on it to make sure it isn't burning. When the crumble is crispy and golden, it is ready.

6. Tastes great with custard or ice cream.

Nutritional Value (Amount per Serving):

Calories: 2509; Fat: 124.91; Carb: 328.12; Protein: 28.45

Air Fryer Carrot Cake

Prep Time: 10 minutes   Cook Time: 35 minutes   Serves: 1

Ingredients:

- 140g of soft brown sugar
- 2 eggs, beaten
- 140g of butter
- 1 orange, zest & juice
- 200g of self-raising flour
- 1tsp of ground cinnamon
- 175g of grated carrot
- 60g of sultanas

Directions:

1. In a bowl, cream together the butter and sugar.
2. Slowly add the beaten eggs.
3. Fold in the flour, a little bit at a time, mixing it as you go. Add the orange juice and zest, grated carrots and sultanas. Gently mix all the ingredients together.
4. Grease the baking tin and pour the mixture in.
5. Place baking tin in the air fryer basket and cook for 35-45 minutes at 175°C. Check on it at 30 minutes and see if the cake has cooked - use a cocktail stick or metal skewer to poke in the middle. If it comes out wet then cook it for a little longer. If the outside is cooking too quickly wrap some foil over the top of the cake. Make sure the foil is secured down so that it doesn't blow about.
6. Remove the baking tin from the air fryer basket and allow to cool for 10 minutes before removing from the tin.
7. Optionally ice with some buttercream.

Nutritional Value (Amount per Serving):

Calories: 2645; Fat: 135.24; Carb: 320.71; Protein: 41.8

Air Fryer Chocolate Chip Cookies

Prep Time: 10 minutes   Cook Time: 35 minutes   Serves: 1

Ingredients:

- 115g of butter, melted
- 55g brown sugar

- 50g caster sugar
- 1 large egg
- 1 tsp of pure vanilla extract
- 185g of plain flour
- 1/2 tsp of bicarbonate of soda
- 1/2 tsp of salt
- 120g of chocolate chips
- 35g of chopped walnuts

Directions:

1. In a medium bowl whisk together melted butter and sugars. Add egg and vanilla and whisk until incorporated. Add flour, bicarbonate of soda, and salt and stir until just combined.
2. Place a small piece of parchment in the basket of an air fryer, making sure there is still room around the edges to allow air flow. Working in batches, use a large cookie scoop, about 3 tablespoons, and scoop dough onto parchment, leaving 5cm between each cookie, press to flatten slightly.
3. Bake in air fryer at 180°C for 8 minutes. Cookies will be golden and slightly soft. Let cool 5 minutes before serving.

Nutritional Value (Amount per Serving):

Calories: 2795; Fat: 150.15; Carb: 332.62; Protein: 34.42

Air Fryer Cookies

Prep Time: 5 minutes   Cook Time: 12 minutes   Serves: 16

Ingredients:

- 150g of salted butter, at room temperature
- 80g of light brown muscovado sugar
- 80g of granulated sugar
- 1 large egg, beaten
- 225g of plain flour
- 1/2 tsp of bicarbonate of soda
- 200g of plain chocolate chips, or chunks

Directions:

1. In a large mixing bowl, beat together the butter, muscovado sugar, granulated sugar, egg, plain flour and bicarbonate of soda to make a firm dough. Add the chocolate chips or chunks and beat again until well incorporated.
2. Using your hands, break off golf ball-sized pieces of the dough and roll them into balls. Continue until all the dough is used up. (If you don't want to cook all the cookies now, transfer a portion to the freezer to cook at a later date.)
3. You can cook the cookies in a large silicone mould or on a sheet of baking paper. Either way, transfer the cookie balls to the air fryer, spacing them out so that they can spread during cooking and bake for 10–12 minutes,

until golden but still fairly soft (they will firm up as they cool). Depending on how many cookies you are cooking off and the size of your air fryer, you may need to do this in several batches. Leave to cool slightly, then serve still slightly warm or cooled. Perfect with a cup of tea or a glass of milk and a smile on your face!

Nutritional Value (Amount per Serving):

Calories: 222; Fat: 11.11; Carb: 28.79; Protein: 2.34

Air Fryer Brownies

Prep Time: 5 minutes   Cook Time: 30 minutes   Serves: 2

Ingredients:

- 100g of caster sugar
- 40g of cocoa powder
- 30g of plain flour
- 1/4 tsp of baking powder
- Pinches of salt
- 60g of butter, melted and cooled slightly
- 1 large egg

Directions:

1. Grease a 15cm round cake pan with cooking spray. In a medium bowl, whisk to combine sugar, cocoa powder, flour, baking powder, and salt.
2. In a small bowl, whisk melted butter and egg until combined. Add wet ingredients to dry ingredients and stir until combined.
3. Transfer brownie batter to prepared cake pan and smooth top. Cook in air fryer at 180°C for 16-18 minutes. Let cool 10 minutes before slicing.

Nutritional Value (Amount per Serving):

Calories: 568; Fat: 27.34; Carb: 76.35; Protein: 6.25

Air Fryer French Toast Sticks

Prep Time: 5 minutes   Cook Time: 30 minutes   Serves: 6

Ingredients:

- 2 large eggs
- 80ml of double cream
- 80ml of whole milk
- 3 tbsp of caster sugar
- 1/4 tsp of ground cinnamon
- 1/2 tsp of vanilla extract
- Salt
- 6 thick slices white loaf or brioche, each slice cut into thirds

- Maple syrup, for serving

Directions:

1. Beat eggs, cream, milk, sugar, cinnamon, vanilla, and a pinch of salt in a large shallow baking dish. Add bread, turn to coat a few times.
2. Arrange French toast in basket of air fryer, working in batches as necessary to not overcrowd basket. Set air fryer to 190°C and cook until golden, about 8 minutes, tossing halfway through.
3. Serve toast warm, drizzled with maple syrup.

Nutritional Value (Amount per Serving):

Calories: 341; Fat: 14.07; Carb: 17.97; Protein: 36.92

Best-Ever Mozzarella Sticks

Prep Time: 5 minutes   Cook Time: 2 hours 20 minutes   Serves: 6

Ingredients:

- 6 mozzarella sticks
- 100g of panko breadcrumbs
- Salt
- Freshly cracked black pepper
- 2 large eggs, well-beaten
- 3 tbsp of plain flour
- Warm marinara, for serving

Directions:

1. Freeze mozzarella sticks until frozen solid, at least 2 hours.
2. After 3 hours, set up a breading station: Place panko, eggs, and flour in 3 separate shallow bowls. Season panko generously with salt and pepper.
3. Coat frozen mozzarella sticks in flour, then dip in egg, then panko, back in the egg, then back in the panko.
4. Arrange frozen breaded mozzarella sticks in an even layer in the basket of your air fryer. Cook on 200°C for 6 minutes, or until golden and crisp on the outside and melty in the centre.
5. Serve with warm marinara sauce for dipping.

Nutritional Value (Amount per Serving):

Calories: 161; Fat: 6.56; Carb: 9.89; Protein: 16.3

Air Fryer Muffins

Prep Time: 10 minutes   Cook Time: 15 minutes   Serves: 6-8

Ingredients:

- 60ml of vegetable oil
- 75g of natural yogurt

- 1 egg
- 2 tbsp of milk
- 100g of golden caster sugar
- 150g of self-raising flour
- 1/4 tsp of bicarbonate of soda
- 75g of blueberries, chocolate chips or dried fruit

Directions:

4. Set the air fryer on 160°C. Mix the oil, yogurt, egg and milk in a large bowl, then fold in the sugar, flour and bicarbonate of soda and combine well. Fold in the blueberries, chocolate chips or dried fruit, if using. Spoon the mixture into silicone cases or an air fryer muffin tin filled with paper cases to three-quarters full. You should be able to make 6-8 muffins, but you may have to bake them in batches.

5. Place the cases or tin in the air fryer basket and cook for 12-15 mins until the muffins are golden brown and a skewer inserted into the centre comes out clean.

Nutritional Value (Amount per Serving):

Calories: 244; Fat: 10.38; Carb: 33.7; Protein: 4.79

APPENDIX RECIPE INDEX

Printed in Great Britain
by Amazon